LEGENDS OF WARFARE
AVIATION

F-4 Phantom II
McDonnell Douglas MiG Hunter

DAVID DOYLE

Schiffer
Military History

4880 Lower Valley Road
Atglen, PA 19310

Designed by Alexa Harris
Cover design by Jack Chappell
Type set in Impact/Minion Pro/Univers LT Std

ISBN: 978-0-7643-6902-5
Printed in India

Published by Schiffer Publishing, Ltd.
4880 Lower Valley Road
Atglen, PA 19310
Phone: (610) 593-1777; Fax: (610) 593-2002
Email: Info@schifferbooks.com
Web: www.schifferbooks.com

For our complete selection of fine books on this and related subjects, please visit our website at www.schifferbooks.com. You may also write for a free catalog.

Schiffer Publishing's titles are available at special discounts for bulk purchases for sales promotions or premiums. Special editions, including personalized covers, corporate imprints, and excerpts, can be created in large quantities for special needs. For more information, contact the publisher.

We are always looking for people to write books on new and related subjects. If you have an idea for a book, please contact us at proposals@schifferbooks.com.

Acknowledgments

This book would not have been possible without the generous assistance and resources of many friends and institutions. Among them, Tom Kailbourn, Dana Bell, Scott Taylor, Marc Levitt and John Higgins at the National Museum of Naval Aviation, Brett Stolle at the National Museum of the United States Air Force, and the National Archives. Most of the photos in this book were scanned by my wife, Denise, without whose help and support this book would not have been possible.

Contents

Introduction

Developed for the United States Navy in the 1950s, the F-4 Phantom II achieved fame and distinction in the hands both of naval aviators and US Air Force (USAF) pilots during the Vietnam War and continued to fly in the forces of the United States and eleven other nations into the 1990s.

Because the Phantom II was initially developed for the Navy, this book will first examine the Navy and Marine Corps variants, while the second half of the book is devoted to USAF variants. Other nations also used the Phantom, which were based on either USN or USAF variants, as most closely aligned with that nation's needs. Those aircraft have been placed in the section that reflects their lineage.

In an interservice combat mission, two Navy F-4Bs of VF-151 drop their bombs on an enemy target in Vietnam under the directions of a US Air Force F-4 of the 13th Tactical Fighter Squadron, 432nd Tactical Reconnaissance Wing, Udorn, Thailand, March 1973. *National Museum of Naval Aviation*

CHAPTER 1
F4H-1F/F-4A

The genesis for the Phantom II came in 1952, when McDonnell Aircraft set out, on its own initiative, to develop an attack fighter for sale to the US Navy. The company's initial efforts were concentrated on enhancing the F3H Demon, and accordingly a proposal was made to the Navy. The Navy had enough interest to order a full-scale mockup but was more interested in a fighter-bomber than in a supersonic fighter.

After design revision to meet its concerns, the Navy issued a letter of intent for a pair of YAH-1 prototypes on October 18, 1954. By mid-1956, however, the requirements had changed again, and the design was again revised, now becoming a two-seat, all-weather, missile-armed interceptor.

On July 25, 1955, the Navy ordered two test aircraft, now designated XF4H-1, and five YF4H-1 service test aircraft on contract NOa(s)55-272. The first flight of the type took place on May 27, 1958, and carrier trials began aboard USS *Independence* on February 15, 1960.

As a result of Secretary of Defense Robert Strange McNamara's push for interservice standardization of aircraft and designations, the USAF looked at the aircraft. Following the type's winning a fly-off against the Convair F-106 Delta Dart, the USAF set out to develop their own version, with emphasis on the fighter-bomber role.

The last of the seven aircraft contracted for in July 1955 was delivered on June 15, 1959. By then, the Navy had already selected the type as the Navy's first-line all-weather fighter of the future. Not quite a month later, the formidable new aircraft was christened the Phantom II.

Since the desired J79-GE-8 engines were not yet available, these aircraft were instead equipped with J79-GE-2 engines, each of which developed 16,150 pounds of static thrust with afterburner.

A total of forty-five of these aircraft, initially designated F4H-1F, were produced. The F suffix was used to indicate the nonstandard (for the type) power plant.

The radar system also differed from the later standard, with the APQ-72 being equipped with a 24-inch rather than a 32-inch reflector.

These aircraft were used in various flight-testing, evaluation, and training programs, rather than being assigned to fleet service. Among those tests were the initial carrier trials, which took place aboard USS *Independence* (CVA-62) on February 15, 1960, using Bureau Number (BuNo) 143391.

Beginning with BuNo 145307, the intake geometry was changed. At 146817 the cockpit was revised and the nose was enlarged, becoming larger and with the pilot sitting markedly higher, improving visibility when landing.

The F4H-1 was redesignated the F-4A on September 18, 1962, as part of the Tri-Service aircraft designation system mandated by Secretary of Defense McNamara.

The F-4 Phantom II had its genesis in McDonnell Aircraft's model 98B / F3H-G, a 1954 concept for a
high-speed fighter with a capacity for heavy munitions. McDonnell produced this mockup of the F3H-G,
which the Navy approved in 1954. *National Museum of Naval Aviation*

The F3H-G was conceived as a single-seat fighter. Originally it was to have two Wright J65 Sapphire engines, license-built copies of the Armstrong-Siddeley Sapphire as used in the FJ-3 Fury. But, owing to trouble in that application, the Navy requested that the engines be changed to General Electric J79s, a new engine not yet in production. The mockup with these engines was designated F3H-H. In Aprll 1955, all work on the J65-powered version was halted. *National Museum of Naval Aviation*

The mockup of the F3H-H illustrated the proposed armament of four 20 mm cannons, mounted two on each side of the fuselage, inboard of the air intakes. Also clear from the point of view was the excellent visibility over the nose of the aircraft. *National Museum of Naval Aviation*

Painted lines indicated the control surfaces on the F3H-H mockup, including the full-span leading-edge flaps and the small trailing-edge flaps. *National Museum of Naval Aviation*

Although the F3H-G/H mockup had only a slight similarity to the F-4 Phantom II, it was a necessary first step in the evolutionary process that would lead to the F-4. In mid-November 1954, the Navy ordered two AH-1 prototypes based on the F3H-G/H. *National Museum of Naval Aviation*

The full-size mockup of the F3H-H, or model 98B, was constructed to showcase two engine options. *On the right*, the J79, and, *on the left*, the significantly smaller J65. *National Museum of Naval Aviation*

A mockup of the F4H-1 was complete by November 1955. The very detailed mockup featured retractable landing gear, folding wings, missile launch rails, and an in-flight refueling probe, which could be extended. However, the mockup had straight wings, but following wind tunnel tests on models, the outer wings of production aircraft were moved upward 12 degrees to improve stability. *National Museum of Naval Aviation*

By the time the AH-1 prototypes were under construction, the Navy had requested that they be built as two-seaters, with a radar intercept officer (RIO) in the rear seat. These prototypes were assigned Bureau Numbers (BuNos) 142259 (*seen here*), and 142260. The Navy redesignated the AH-1 prototypes as the YF4H-1 on June 23, 1955, and later it was redesignated the F4H-1F. *National Museum of Naval Aviation*

The F4H-1 142259 was rolled out of the McDonnell Aircraft plant reveals on May 27, 1958. The aircraft was quite similar in appearance to the ultimate F-4 Phantom II, with some exceptions: it had a shorter nose equipped with a test probe; lower canopies, with the top of the rear canopy extending in a straight line with the top of the fuselage behind it; a forward-curving upper edge on each engine-air intake; and NACA scoops for the air-conditioning system above the nose gear instead of the raised scoops used on production Phantoms. *Naval History and Heritage Command*

The F4H-1 made the Phantom II's maiden flight, with test pilot Robert C. Little at the controls, the same day it was rolled out. A McDonnell press release at the time stated that 6,800 man-years of labor had gone into the project prior to that flight. *National Museum of Naval Aviation*

On final approach, the leading- and trailing-edge flaps, as well as the landing gear, are down on F4H-1 142259. This aircraft made five test flights from Lambert Field in St. Louis before being ferried to Edwards Air Force Base (AFB) by way of Tinker and Kirtland on June 23, 1958.

After completing a series of test flights starting in May 1958, F4H-1, BuNo 142259, was used in Project Top Flight, an attempt to set a new altitude record. During one such flight on October 21, 1959, the plane crashed, killing test pilot Gerald "Zeke" Huelsbeck. *National Museum of Naval Aviation*

After the crash of F4H-1 142259, the second prototype, 142260, was used in Project Top Flight, and Cmdr. Lawrence E. Flint Jr. set a new world's altitude record of 98,560 feet with this plane on December 6, 1959, beating a previous Soviet record by 3,902 feet. *National Museum of Naval Aviation*

The name Phantom II was officially bestowed on the F4H-1 series of aircraft on July 3, 1959, and this example, BuNo 143391, one of five preproduction planes (BuNos 143388–143392), is marked with the new name. The leading-edge wing flaps are lowered. *National Museum of Naval Aviation*

F4H-1 143391 has just landed on USS *Independence* (CVA-62) during carrier-suitability trials in February 1960. The top of the aft canopy was in a straight line with the top of the fuselage, resulting in poor all-around and especially rearward vision for the RIO. *National Museum of Naval Aviation*

The first forty-five production F4H-1s left the assembly line with General Electric J79-GE-2 or -2A engines, and on May 1, 1961, these forty-five planes were redesignated F4H-1Fs to distinguish them from later Phantoms with J79-GE-8 engines. Seen here is F4H-1F 146817. *National Museum of Naval Aviation*

An F4H-1 demonstrates its munitions-carrying capacity by flying with a large load of red-painted inert Mk. 82 500-pound bombs. These planes now were equipped with an AAA-4 infrared sensor under the nose; as a test plane, this one has a long probe mounted on the nose. *National Museum of Naval Aviation*

McDonnell F4H-1 145307 of
Fighter Squadron 101 (VF-101) set
a new low-altitude speed record,
at an average of 902.76 miles per
hour over a 3-kilometer course
during Project Sageburner at
White Sands, New Mexico, in
July 1961. *National Museum of
Naval Aviation*

The second YF4H-1 prototype,
BuNo 142260, appears in markings
for Project Skyburner, a 1961 effort
to capture the speed record. On
December 22 of that year, Lt. Col.
Robert B. Robinson (USMC) set
the new record, 1,606.347 miles
per hour, in 142260. *National
Museum of Naval Aviation*

The F4H-1Fs were redesignated F-4A in September 1962. An example assigned to Composite Squadron 7 (VC-7), BuNo 148258, is seen in flight over the Southern California coast around 1968 with two squadron mates representing, along with the Phantom II, mainstays of the US Navy's carrier-based combat aircraft in the 1960s: a Vought F-8 Crusader fighter and a Douglas A-4 Skyhawk attack plane. *National Museum of Naval Aviation*

Aircraft 145310 is shown here with a display of all the external stores the aircraft was equipped to accommodate, ranging from the twenty-four 250-pound Mk. 81 General Purpose bombs in the foreground to external fuel tanks, chemical bombs, and auxiliary power pod near the aircraft. *National Museum of Naval Aviation*

CHAPTER 2
F4H-1/F-4B

Contracts continued to be issued to McDonnell for further-refined aircraft. Beginning with block 6 and the forty-eighth aircraft, the J79-GE-8A engines—developing 10,000 lbs. of thrust dry and 17,000 lbs. with afterburner—began to be used, and the "F" suffix was dropped from the model designation. The engine change came along with revised air intakes. The F4H-1 aircraft of block 6, beginning with BuNo 148363, were considered the first fully operational versions of the aircraft. That aircraft took to the air for the first time on March 25, 1961, with test pilot Thomas Harris at the controls.

On September 18, 1962, this aircraft too was redesignated, becoming the F-4B. Externally, the F-4B strongly resembled the late F-4A, with raised canopies and enlarged radomes housing APQ-72 radar systems. However, they were equipped with an Aero-27A ejector rack on the fuselage centerline, which could accommodate a 600-gallon drop tank, plus eight additional hardpoints, four under the fuselage and four under the wings, allowing it to carry up to 16,000 pounds of ordnance.

Internally, the F-4B was equipped with the AJB-3 nuclear-bombing system and AN/ASA-32 autopilot and flight control system. An APR-30 radar-homing/warning system was installed on each F-4B.

The initial deliveries of F4H-1s went to VF-121, a training unit at Miramar, which received its aircraft in early 1961, followed quickly by additional deliveries to another training unit, VF-101, based in Oceana.

The first operational units to be equipped with the new aircraft were VF-74, also at Oceana, and VF-114, based at Miramar, both of which were equipped in mid-1961.

Although McDonnell had originally proposed a photo-reconnaissance variant of the Phantom II, the Navy expressed no interest in it—until 1962. By that time, the Air Force was planning on procuring Phantoms, including the RF-110A, which had night reconnaissance capabilities that were lacking in the Navy's then-standard recon aircraft, the F8U-1P.

The Navy expressed an interested in an aircraft similar to the RF-110A, with the Navy variant being designated the F4H-1P. In February 1963, nine such aircraft, by then designated RF-4B, were ordered for the Marine Corps.

Like the more plentiful USAF RF-4C (as the RF-110A had been redesignated in September 1962), the RF-4B was unarmed. Its nose was 4 feet, 8 7/8 inches longer than that of the standard F-4B. The long nose housed a small Texas Instruments AN/APQ-99 forward-looking radar setup for terrain following and terrain avoidance and could also be used for ground mapping, as well as three camera bays. Those bays were designated stations 1, 2, and 3. Station 1 housed a single forward oblique or vertical KS-87 camera, while station 2 carried a single KA-87 low-altitude camera. Station 3 normally carried a single KA-55A or KA-91 high-altitude panoramic camera but could be equipped with the much-larger KS-91 or KS-127A camera. The aircraft was configured such that the film could be processed in flight and film cassettes ejected at

The first operational model of the Phantom II was the F4H-1. While flying with the F4H-1 designation at the time this October 1961 photo of BuNo 148373 of VF-74 was taken, a year later all F4H-1 aircraft from block 6 and up had been redesignated the F-4B. The earlier (first forty-seven) F4H-1 aircraft were redesignated F-4A at that time. On the vertical tail is the "AJ" code for Carrier Air Group Six (CAG-6), based on USS *Forrestal* (CV-59). *National Museum of Naval Aviation*

low altitude, to provide troops on the ground with up-to-date intelligence. For night work, provision was made to eject photoflash cartridges upward from either side of the photo Phantom. The rear cockpit housed the reconnaissance systems operator.

That operator was tasked with operating the suite of electronic gear, including an AN/APQ-102 side-looking mapping radar, the antenna for which was faired into the lower fuselage just ahead of the intakes. Behind the AN/APQ-102 was the AN/AAD-4 infrared reconnaissance system. Faired into both sides of the vertical fin was the antenna for an ARC-105 transceiver. Also aboard the aircraft was a Litton ASN-48 inertial navigation system, an ASW-25B one-way data link, and ALQ-126 deceptive ECM system.

The first flight of the RF-4B was on March 12, 1965, with unit deliveries beginning in May, when VMCJ-3 at MCAS El Toro began receiving aircraft. This was rapidly followed by deliveries to VMCJ-2 at MCAS Cherry Point and to VMCJ-1 at Iwakuni in Japan, the latter of which were deployed to Đà Nẵng in October 1966.

Carrier deployment of the Phantom began in late 1962, with VF-102 aboard USS *Enterprise* (CVAN-65) while on her shakedown cruise. Almost simultaneously, VF-74, the first Phantom unit to be carrier qualified, deployed to the Mediterranean aboard USS *Forrestal* (CVA-59), from which they operated until March 1963.

The first combat operations of the Phantom occurred on August 5, 1964, when VF-142 and VF-143 flew top cover for Operation Pierce Arrow from USS *Constellation* (CVA-64). The first Phantom air-to-air kill was reported to have occurred on April 9, 1965, when Lt. (jg) Terence Murphy, flying VF-96 F-4B (BuNo 151403) from USS *Ranger*, downed a Chinese MiG-17 near Hainan Island. Unfortunately, Murphy, his back seater, and his aircraft were lost in the engagement as well.

Just over two months later, on June 17, 1965, Cmdr. Thomas C. Page and Lt. Jon C. Smith Jr. of VF-21, flying F-4B 151488 from USS *Midway* (CVA-41), shot down a North Vietnamese MiG-17 near Haiphong.

The Marines began taking deliveries of the F-4B in June 1962, and starting in April 1965, Marine Phantoms were based in Vietnam and Thailand, as well as aboard USS *America* (CVA-66).

Ultimately, 649 F-4B aircraft were delivered to the Navy and Marine Corps, the last of these deliveries being in March 1967.

F-4B-26-MC, BuNo153008 and modex 203, served with VF-111 on USS *Coral Sea* (CVA-43). The last two digits of the modex, 03, are at the top of the dorsal fin. The wing had a highly polished surface, with the reflection of "NAVY" appearing on it. *National Museum of Naval Aviation*

Landing gear lowered, an F-4B assigned to VF-96 and piloted by Lt. Cmdr. Kenneth W. Stecker (USN) is about to fly under the Golden Gate Bridge on October 19, 1962. Carrier Air Group Nine's code, NG, is on the vertical tail. Stecker was the executive officer (XO) of VF-96. *National Museum of Naval Aviation*

Arguably, the honors for the classiest tail squadron colors for the Phantom IIs go to VF-111 "Sundowners," based on USS *Coral Sea*. Here, F-4B-13-MC, BuNo 150466, unloads a stick of bombs on an enemy target during a mission on November 25, 1966. *National Museum of Naval Aviation*

An F-4B assigned to VF-31 is about to touch down on USS *Saratoga* (CVA-60) on October 26, 1964. This squadron had transitioned to the Phantom earlier that year. In the foreground are two Phantoms and a North American RA-5C Vigilante. *National Museum of Naval Aviation*

The 1962 redesignation of F4H-1s to F-4Bs also included the addition of production-block numbers and an "MC" for McDonnell suffix to the designation. Here are F-4B-8-MC 148415 of VMF(AW)-513 and F-4B-13-MC 150468 of VMF(AW)-314, July 1963. *National Museum of Naval Aviation*

Tailhook lowered, an F-4B of VF-21 returns to USS *Midway* (CVA-41) after an airstrike on North Vietnam while, *in the foreground*, a landing-signal officer (LSO), Lt. Vernon Jumper, gives last-minute instructions to the pilot to guide him to deck. *National Museum of Naval Aviation*

This F-4B, BuNo 152218, of VF-21, based on USS *Midway* (CVA-41), executes a mission over Vietnam in 1965. An AIM-7 Sparrow missile is on the left pylon: an unusual configuration. In addition, two AIM-9 Sidewinder missiles are mounted on the right pylon. *National Museum of Naval Aviation*

The catapult bridle is attached to an F-4B of VF-121 on USS *Constellation* (CVA-64) on August 5, 1968. The leading-edge flaps are lowered; these flaps helped effect boundary-layer control by means of high-pressure air blown over them. *National Museum of Naval Aviation*

F-4B-11-MC, BuNo 149472, assigned to Marine Fighter Attack Squadron 122 (VMFA-122), is parked on a hardstand at Naval Air Station (NAS) Miramar, California, around 1966. The two-letter "DC" code of VMFA-122 is on the vertical tail. *National Museum of Naval Aviation*

F-4B Phantom IIs from VF-96 and an unidentified USMC unit are parked on the flight deck of USS *Enterprise* (CVAN-65) on June 21, 1966. The planes of VF-96 are marked with the two-letter code of Carrier Air Wing Nine, NG, on their vertical tails.

Two US Navy F-4B Phantom IIs fly in close formation over the Gulf of Tonkin in September 1968. They were assigned to VF-142 and were armed for air-to-air combat with Sidewinder and Sparrow missiles. *National Museum of Naval Aviation*

An F-4B of VF-96, based on USS *Enterprise*, pummels Viet Cong positions with unguided air-to-ground rockets from pods underneath the wings during a mission in April 1966. This plane was F-4B-23-MC, BuNo 152283. A small "2" is on top of the rudder. *National Museum of Naval Aviation*

F-4B-20-MC, BuNo 152212, of VF-114, Carrier Air Wing 11, has just caught an arrestor wire during a landing on USS *Kitty Hawk* (CVA-63) on March 25, 1969. In the background are an RA-5C Vigilante (*left*), two more Phantoms, and an A-7 Corsair II. *National Museum of Naval Aviation*

Navy F-4B, serial number 150466, flying with VF-111 "Sundowners" from the carrier USS *Coral Sea* unleashes its load of bombs over North Vietnam on March 8, 1972. In the background, a second *Coral Sea* Phantom likewise sends its bombs hurtling downward; that aircraft was assigned to VF-51, the "Screaming Eagles." *National Museum of Naval Aviation*

"California Dreaming" was the nickname of this F-4B-25MC, BuNo 152991, with markings for VF-51 from USS *Coral Sea* when the photo was taken on July 22, 1972, at NAS Alameda, California. The plane's skin joints had been sealed for long-term storage. *National Museum of Naval Aviation*

F-4B, BuNo 153070, of Tactical Electronic Warfare Squadron Thirty-Three (VAQ-33), "the Firebirds," flies along a coastline around April 1973. The acronym "FEWSG" stood for Fleet Electronic Warfare Support Group, at NAS Norfolk, Virginia. *National Museum of Naval Aviation*

An F-4B assigned to VF-51 comes in for a landing at NAS Miramar, California, on January 22, 1974. The leading-edge flaps are lowered, as are the trailing-edge flaps, providing excellent lift when the plane was flying at low speeds. *National Museum of Naval Aviation*

In the early 1960s, a reconnaissance version of the F-4, the RF-4B, was produced, with all forty-six of them going to the Marine Corps. This plane was similar to the US Air Force's RF-4C and was equipped with a specially designed nose loaded with photoreconnaissance equipment. RF-4B-26-MC 153105 of Marine Composite Reconnaissance Squadron 1 (VMCJ-1) is seen at a base in South Vietnam in 1968. EF-10D Skyknights are visible behind the Phantom. *National Museum of Naval Aviation*

Two technicians position a vertical still camera on the rear door of the camera bay of an RF-4B serving with Marine Composite Reconnaissance Squadron 2 (VMCJ-2). Warning stencils, mostly for radiation hazards, are plentiful on the aircraft. *National Museum of Naval Aviation*

Parked on a hardstand at NAS North Island (NORIS), San Diego, California, around 1969 is the McDonnell RF-4B with US Navy BuNo 153099, assigned to VMCJ-2. It was marked with modex 6 and a Playboy bunny logo on the rudder. *National Museum of Naval Aviation*

A crane is ready to remove RF-4B-21-MC 151979 of VMCJ-3 from the runway at Marine Corps Air Station (MCAS) Santa Ana, California, following a crash on July 30, 1969. This plane would be repaired and go on to serve with the Marine Corps into the 1980s. *National Museum of Naval Aviation*

A formation of photoreconnaissance Phantoms of Marine Composite Reconnaissance Squadron 3 around 1970 includes RF-4B-23-MC 151983 (*in the foreground*). The center plane in the background is RF-4B-24-MC 153092. *National Museum of Naval Aviation*

RF-4B-41-MC 157344 of VMCJ-2 is parked on a hardstand at MCAS El Toro, California, on June 5, 1975. The last four digits of the plane's BuNo, 7344, are marked in large numerals on the rear part of the fuselage. *National Museum of Naval Aviation*

RF-4B-43-MC 157350, the next-to-last RF-4B to be produced, is assigned to VMCJ-2 and seen here at MacDill AFB, Florida, in August 1971. To the right is a USAF type A/M32A-60 generator set, often called the "dash-60 start cart." *National Museum of Naval Aviation*

Four RF-4Bs fly in formation in about 1976. The nearest three planes are marked for Marine Tactical Reconnaissance Squadron 3 (VMFP-3), but each one has a different unit code on the tail. The farthest RF-4B was from VMCJ-1, with the correct RM squadron code. *National Museum of Naval Aviation*

McDonnell RF-4B-41-MC, BuNo 157346, displays markings for VMFP-3, assigned to USS *Midway*, in this photo dated December 17, 1977. An electronic-countermeasures antenna is mounted on the upper part of the engine-air intake. *National Museum of Naval Aviation*

During 1976, RF-4B-26-MC 153101 of VMFP-3 bears special markings in celebration of the US bicentennial, including red, white, and blue numbering and squadron designation and a circle of stars around the RF tail code. *National Museum of Naval Aviation*

Like many other US military aircraft, RF-4B-26-MC 153101 of VMFP-3 received special patriotic decorations during the 1976 bicentennial, including a "Spirit of America" banner and crossed flags on the tail. *National Museum of Naval Aviation*

Trouble struck RF-4B-21-MC 151979, seen in an earlier photo, again when it suffered nose-gear failure and crashed into a barrier on USS *Midway* on January 25, 1984. The plane was severely damaged and subsequently was written off as unrepairable. *National Museum of Naval Aviation*

The final RF-4B to be produced was RF-4B-43-MC 157351, seen here in markings for VMFP-3 at MCAS El Toro, California, on July 10, 1990. The plane, including the centerline drop tank, was painted overall in a dark- or navy-blue scheme. *National Museum of Naval Aviation*

CHAPTER 3

F-4G (Navy)

F-4G, BuNo 150484, assigned to VF-213 "Black Lions," approaches the catapult on an aircraft carrier, likely USS *Kitty Hawk*, around early June 1966. In the background is another F-4G, BuNo 1560642, with a similar two-tone-green camouflage paint scheme. *National Museum of Naval Aviation*

In 1963, the Navy equipped thirteen F-4Bs for fleet air defense through the installation of a ground control system similar to SAGE. The two-way data link coupled the autopilots of these aircraft to controllers aboard ships or other aircraft.

The program began with the fitting of F-4B BuNo 148254 with an AN/ASW-13 two-way data-link communication system and approach power compensator. The autopilot of the aircraft was modified such that inputs from the data link could actuate the flight controls, while the approach power compensator controlled the throttles while the aircraft as landing. To make space for all the new gear, the capacity of the number 1 fuel tank was reduced. The rear cockpit was revised to incorporate additional control boxes and indicators, while the front cockpit was fitted with indicator lights and a button that the pilot could push to acknowledge that the data from the controller was received. With the initial tests favorable, the ASW-13 was replaced with an AN/ASW-21, which added the capability to relay weapons, fuel, and oxygen status to the controller.

That controller, aboard ship, was using AN/SPN-10 radar and an AN/USC-1 data link. Following successful tests with BuNo 148254, twelve further aircraft were similarly modified while on the assembly line. These aircraft were BuNos 150481, 150484, 150487, 150489, 150492, 150625, 150629, 150633, 150636, 150639, 150642, and 150645, which differed from the pilot plane in that they were equipped with a retractable radar reflector just ahead of the nosewheel, which allowed the shipboard equipment to better track the Phantom as it was landing. The first of these production aircraft took to the sky on March 20, 1963. Two of the aircraft, BuNos 150489 and 150625, were assigned to NATC (Naval Air Training Command) Patuxent for additional testing, and the remainder were assigned to VF-96 at Miramar. In early 1964 the VF-96 aircraft were transferred to VF-213. On March 31, 1964, the modified aircraft were designated F-4G, not to be confused with the later USAF F-4G Wild Weasel.

From October 19, 1965, to June 13, 1966, the F-4Gs were aboard *Kitty Hawk* in the Gulf of Tonkin, during which time BuNo 150645 was shot down by North Vietnamese antiaircraft artillery (AAA). After their return to the US, the F-4Gs were modified to F-4B configuration. However, the later F-4J was equipped with a similar data-link system that permitted automatic landings.

The US Navy converted thirteen F-4Bs to F-4Gs (not to be confused with the USAF model F-4G, used for Wild Weasel anti-SAM operations) by equipping them with a two-way data-link system to enable operators on ships to control the planes during interceptions. The F-4s also had the capability for automatically controlled night and all-weather carrier landings. This example is BuNo 150636 in the markings of VF-116, a squadron for which there seems to be no record. *National Museum of Naval Aviation*

Two F-4Gs of VF-213 "Black Lions" are prepared to catapult from USS *Kitty Hawk* (CVA-63) during that carrier's October 1965–June 1966 deployment to Vietnam. These planes have an experimental USN camouflage scheme featuring two shades of green. *National Museum of Naval Aviation*

F-4G, BuNo 150642, of VF-213 touches down on USS *Kitty Hawk* after a mission during the squadron's 1965–66 deployment to Vietnam. The modex 102 is painted on the nose, and the last digit of the number, 2, is on the nose-gear door and the rudder. *National Museum of Naval Aviation*

Details of the markings of the green-camouflaged F-4Gs based on *Kitty Hawk* are visible in this photo of BuNo 150492. The BuNo and "NAVY" were in black, and the last digit, 4, of the modex, 104, was in white on the rudder and the flap. In the foreground is the tail of F-4B-24-MC, BuNo 152325, in the markings of VF-114. *National Museum of Naval Aviation*

F-4G, BuNo 150642, of the VF-213 "Black Lions," tugs on the arrestor wire after landing aboard USS *Kitty Hawk*, in early June 1966. The last digit of the Bureau Number, "2," is painted on the flaps. *National Museum of Naval Aviation*

After serving with VF-213 on USS *Kitty Hawk* during a deployment to the Gulf of Tonkin from 1965 to 1966, F-4G 150642 was transferred to VF-121. The plane is seen in markings for that squadron at NAS Miramar, California, in September 1966. *National Museum of Naval Aviation*

The experimental green camouflage is seen on another F-4G, BuNo 150642, assigned to VF-121, in a photo taken at NAS Miramar, California, on September 17, 1966. The undersides were gloss white, and the frame of the pilot's canopy appears to be gray. *National Museum of Naval Aviation*

In large part on the basis of feedback from the fleet concerning the F-4B, the Navy requested changes to the Phantom, which resulted in a new model—the F-4J. The F-4J would be the final Phantom model built new for the Navy by McDonnell.

Three F-4Bs, BuNos 151473, 151496, and 151497, were modified to incorporate the new features, becoming YF-4J test articles. The first YF-4J flight was June 4, 1965, and the first flight of a production F-4J was on May 27, 1966.

The F-4J differed from the F-4B in several ways, notably including new, more-powerful engines, the J79-GE-10. These engines developed 17,900 pounds of thrust each in afterburner and have longer afterburner turkey feathers than the earlier -8 engines. The F-4J also had more-robust landing gear with larger main landing-gear wheels. The larger wheels required that the upper and lower panels of the inner wings be bulged, similarly to those of the Air Force F-4C. Incidentally, this type of landing gear and wings was also used on the final twelve RF-4Bs produced, BuNos 153114, 153115, and 157342/157351.

Internally, the size of the number 1 fuel cell was reduced to allow more space for avionics, but an additional fuel cell installed in the rear fuselage more than offset this, raising the internal fuel capacity to 1,998 gallons.

A slot was added to the stabilator leading edge, and the inboard leading edge was locked in the up position. These changes allowed a large leading-edge down deflection without stalling. This and a change to the aileron settings allowed a 144 mph approach speed as compared to 157 mph for the F-4B.

A larger radome was installed, housing the AN/AWG-10 fire control system, featuring AN/APG-59 pulse-Doppler radar. This system would detect and track low-flying aircraft. Internally, ground attack capabilities were improved through the installation of the AN/AJB-7 bombing system. Automatic carrier landings were made possible through the installation of an AN/ASW-25 one-way data link, building on the experiences with the F-4G.

F-4J deliveries began on October 1, 1966, with VF-101 transitioning to the type in December. Both Navy and Marine Corps units, with few exceptions, replaced their F-4Bs with the F-4Js, with the first USMC unit, VMFA-334, getting their F-4Js in June 1967.

As with the earlier F-4B, the F-4J saw extensive use in Vietnam. On September 11, 1972, the VMFA-333 crew, Maj. Thomas Lasseter and Capt. John D. Commings, flying from USS *America* (CV-66), shot down a North Vietnamese MiG-21 with F-4J BuNo 155526. This was the only USMC air-to-air victory during the war.

From January 1969 through the end of the 1973 season, the Blue Angels flight demonstration team flew modified F-4Js. The team switched to the smaller and more fuel-efficient A-4 Skyhawk because of the Arab oil embargo.

Before production of the F-4J halted in January 1972, with 522 produced, several further improvements were added to the model and also retrofitted to existent F-4Js, including provision for carrying upgraded Sidewinder missiles, the addition of Visual Target Acquisition System (VTAS) helmet sight, Sanders AN/ALQ-126 electronics countermeasures set, an AN/AYK-14 dogfight computer, AN/APR-32 radar-warning set, and reduced-smoke J79-GE-10B engines.

In 1984, fifteen low-flight-time F-4Js were sold to the British and modified at Naval Air Station (NAS) North Island to bring them closer to the standard British Phantom configuration, additional quantities of which would be cost prohibitive to new build in such low numbers. The aircraft were assigned the RAF serials ZE350/ZE364 and were assigned to No. 74(F) Squadron.

The F-4J was in effect an improved version of the F-4B, with strengthened landing gear and other upgrades and changes. This model had the J79-GE-10 engines, with longer afterburner "turkey feathers" than on preceding models of the Phantom II. The F-4J's stabilators had slotted leading edges for better low-speed performance. Here, an F-4J of VF-102 "Diamondbacks" runs up its engines a moment away from launching from USS *America* (CVA-66) in 1968. *National Museum of Naval Aviation*

On a mission over Vietnam on February 9, 1972, F-4J-35-MC 155800 of VF-96 shows its undersides, including bulges in the wings to accommodate the larger landing gear. This model of Phantom lacked the infrared sensor pod underneath the nose. *National Museum of Naval Aviation*

An F-4J-35-MC of VF-96, BuNo 155787, is being refueled from a Douglas EKA-3B over the Gulf of Tonkin on February 9, 1972. The US Navy's Phantom IIs had retractable refueling probes to the right side of the cockpit. *National Museum of Naval Aviation*

F-4J-35-MC, BuNo 155799, of VF-92 is prepared for launching from USS *Constellation* in the Gulf of Tonkin in May 1972, while in the background is F-4J-35-MC 155799 of VF-96. Artwork to the rear of the cockpit is of a hand of cards and multicolored spades. *National Museum of Naval Aviation*

During a raid on enemy forces in Vietnam in about 1972, F-4J-34-MC, BuNo 155573, of VF-96 "Fighting Falcons" releases a load of 500-pound bombs. The tail of another Phantom is visible in the background above the fuselage of this plane. *National Museum of Naval Aviation*

F-4J-35-MC, BuNo155792, of VF-96 has the catapult bridle attached and is about to be launched from USS *Constellation* on a raid on Vietnam in May 1972. The "NG" code for Carrier Air Wing Nine is emblazoned on the vertical tail. *National Museum of Naval Aviation*

Navy Phantom IIs assigned to VF-96 drop 500-pound bombs during a mission over Vietnam in 1972. In the foreground is F-4J-35-MC, BuNo 155800, while the middle plane is F-4J-35-MC 15579. The planes were based on USS *Constellation*. *National Museum of Naval Aviation*

Loaded with 500-pound bombs and Sparrow and Sidewinder missiles, an F-4J, modex 206, of VF-92 is ready for the next mission over Vietnam on December 1, 1972. The plane was then based aboard USS *Constellation* (CVA-64). *National Museum of Naval Aviation*

An F-4J of VF-96 hits a barricade on USS *Constellation* on February 26, 1973. If a normal carrier landing by tail hook and arrestor wire was not possible, a webbing barricade was set up between stanchions to stop the plane. *National Museum of Naval Aviation*

Two F-4Js of VF-143 "Pukin' Dogs" fly over their carrier, USS *Enterprise* (CVAN-65), in the South China Sea on September 31, 1971. The nearer plane has the last four digits of its BuNo, 5773, on the fuselage; the other has 5766. Each plane has a large squadron insignia painted on the side of the fuselage, aft of the engine-air intake, as well as a horizontal red stripe on the upper part of the fuselage from the aft cockpit to near the front of the stabilator. *National Museum of Naval Aviation*

This F-4J-32-MC, BuNo 153882, of VF-92 and assigned to USS *Constellation* exhibited colorful markings when photographed at NAS Miramar in late October 1973. Superimposed on the yellow vertical tail is the squadron's "Silver Kings" emblem. *National Museum of Naval Aviation*

Tail hook and wing flaps lowered, an F-4J of VF-92 approaches USS *Constellation* for landing on August 28, 1974. The tip of the centerline drop tank is painted in yellow like the vertical tail; the air-conditioner air scoop aft of the radome is painted black. *National Museum of Naval Aviation*

F-4J-47-MC 158378 was the next-to-last F-4J produced. It is seen in markings for VF-21, based on USS *Ranger* (CVA-61) on January 22, 1974, over Southern California, and it was the personal aircraft of Commander Attack Carrier Air Wing Two. *National Museum of Naval Aviation*

McDonnell F4J, BuNo 158362, seen here sometime between 1973 and 1975, served with VF-154 aboard USS *Ranger*. The modex was 111, but only the last two digits are marked at the top of the dorsal fin. *National Museum of Naval Aviation*

Phantoms of Fighter Squadron 96 are lined up along the flight deck of the aircraft carrier USS *Constellation* during operations in the South China Sea on August 28, 1974. The nearest plane is F-4J-35-MC, BuNo 155805, with the squadron's falcon symbol on the drop tank. *National Museum of Naval Aviation*

F-4J-46-MC, BuNo 158365, of VF-21 "Freelancers" flies high over Scarborough Shoal in the South China Sea in September 1974. This Phantom was based on USS *Ranger* at that time. Fighter Squadron 21 began flying F-4Js in 1968. *National Museum of Naval Aviation*

In another photograph of F-4J-46-MC, BuNo 158365, of VF-21 over Scarborough Shoal in September 1974, an aircraft carrier, possibly USS *Ranger*, is visible below the front end of the drop tank on the plane's centerline pylon. *National Museum of Naval Aviation*

In a 1974 photograph looking forward from the bridge of USS *Constellation* (CVA-64), in the foreground are three F-4Js: BuNo 155580 and modex 100 of VF-96; 153842/205 of VF-92; and 153819/112 of VF-92. *In the background*, a Phantom II approaches the starboard catapult while another Phantom has just launched from that catapult. Ready for launch from the port catapult is a Douglas RA-3B Skywarrior. *National Museum of Naval Aviation*

McDonnell F-4J-35-MC 155792 comes in for a landing on USS *Constellation* on August 28, 1974. In the preceding photograph, this plane is the third one in the line. On the nose is the modex, 107. Parked in the foreground is F-4J-34-MC, BuNo 155768. *National Museum of Naval Aviation*

Another VF-96 Phantom, F-4J-35-MC 555787, flies a mission from USS *Constellation* around October 1974. The modex of this plane, 104, is marked in black with white shadowing on the side of the nose. Two bombs are on the left pylon. *National Museum of Naval Aviation*

Somewhere in the Indian Ocean in November 1974, an F-4J-30-MC, BuNo 153819, assigned to VF-96 launches from catapult no. 4 on USS *Constellation*. On the nose of the Phantom is the modex, 112. The plane carries Sidewinder missiles on the pylons. *National Museum of Naval Aviation*

F-4J-46-MC 158359 of VF-21 and another Phantom, the tail of which is just visible to the upper right, fly in close formation over Southern California in December 1974. The modex on the nose of the aircraft in the foreground, 205, is black, with yellow shadowing. *National Museum of Naval Aviation*

F-4J-33-MC 155558 of VF-171 is poised on catapult no. 1 on the deck of the carrier USS *Forrestal* (CV-59) preparatory to launching. The aircraft's modex, 178, can be seen on the lowered right flap. Parked to the left is an F-14 Tomcat. *National Museum of Naval Aviation*

US bicentennial markings adorn F-4J-30-MC 153817 of VF-191 in October 1976. On the top of the intake is a defensive-countermeasures (DECM) antenna. This plane was lost on November 15, 1976, after engine failure during a night launch. *National Museum of Naval Aviation*

F-4J-35-MC 155807 of VMFA-122 "Werewolves" is parked at MCAS Miramar on June 5, 1976. The two-letter "DC" code was particular to VMFA-122, and the cross on the tail is part of the squadron's emblem. A DECM antenna is on the upper part of the intake. *National Museum of Naval Aviation*

US bicentennial markings are on F-4J-33-MC, BuNo 155521, from VMFA-451 in a June 14, 1976, photograph. These markings include "1776–1976" in red, white, and blue numerals on the fuselage above the wing. The canopy frames are dark blue. *National Museum of Naval Aviation*

A portion of the right side of F-4J-41-MC 157266 is viewed close up. Under the pylon is what appears to be a travel pod: a streamlined container for carrying crew baggage. The pod is not attached to release shackles but instead is fitted to a frame bolted to the pylon. *National Museum of Naval Aviation*

The numerous stencils on the middle and forward parts of the fuselage and the inboard pylon on the left side of an F-4J are visible in this photograph. They include information on systems inside access panels, caution and warning notices, and attachment points. *National Museum of Naval Aviation*

More of the midsection of the F-4J and its stencils is depicted. To the upper right is a hook-shaped symbol indicating the location of a hoist hook; a similar symbol is toward the left. Also in view is a Sidewinder missile launch rail on the side of the pylon. *National Museum of Naval Aviation*

Aviation artist Keith Ferris was influential in instituting low-visibility camouflage on US military aircraft. This F-4J-32-MC, BuNo 153879, of VF-194, photographed at NAS Miramar in late 1976, wears such a scheme designed by Ferris in the mid-1970s. *National Museum of Naval Aviation*

Three F-4Js of VF-33, Carrier Air Wing Six, from USS *Independence* exhibit varying camouflage schemes and markings in a photo taken in about 1979. The plane to the right has a low-visibility paint job and markings, including small national insignia. *National Museum of Naval Aviation*

In the foreground is F-4J-29-MC 153783, part of a small lot of F-4Js transferred in the 1980s to the Royal Air Force. It was renumbered with RAF serial ZE352. All these planes served with No. 74(F) Squadron. The squadron's insignia, versions of which are on the vertical tail and the fuselage below the windscreen, featured a tiger's head; King George VI approved the insignia for the squadron in 1937. Accompanying this plane is an F-4S of VF-301. *National Museum of Naval Aviation*

An export version of the Phantom II, designated the F-4K by the US and the Phantom FG Mk. 1 by the British, was produced for the Royal Navy. Essentially, it was an F-4J airframe with Rolls-Royce Spey engines. Here, FG Mk. 1 XV588 is about to be launched. *National Museum of Naval Aviation*

The first export customer for the Phantom was the Royal Navy, with the service initially ordering 143 of the aircraft, which, while based on the F-4J, were considerably modified for British use. These aircraft were designated F-4K by McDonnell, and Phantom FG.1 by the Royal Navy.

However, cancellation of the planned expansion of the Royal Navy carrier fleet in 1966 led to a reduction in the size of the order. In 1968, the British government announced plans not only to phase out fixed-wing aviation, but to decommission all its carriers by 1972. This led to the order for Phantoms to be reduced even further, to twenty-eight. Ultimately, twelve of those aircraft were assigned to *Ark Royal*, which had been modified to accommodate the Phantom. In 1970, it was decided to retain the *Ark Royal* in use, and the 892 NAS operated the F-4K from her decks until she was finally withdrawn in 1978.

At that time, the F-4Ks were transferred to No. 111 Squadron RAF, where they operated alongside the 116 FGR.2 or F-4M aircraft ordered by that branch. Earlier, twenty F-4Ks had been acquired as a result of Royal Navy cancellations, those being assigned to No. 43 Squadron.

Both the F-4K and the F-4M were powered by Rolls-Royce RB.168-15R Spey 201 turbofans, each developing 12,250 lb.s.t. dry and 20,515 lb.s.t. with afterburner. The new engines required that the aft fuselage be redesigned. Internally, many of the avionics were replaced with a similar system of UK origin.

The F-4M had antiskid brakes, which the F-4K lacked, and the fire control system differed between the models as well. Neither model had an internal cannon, but the F-4M could accommodate the SUU-16/A and SUU-23/A gun pods.

Initially intended for use both in ground attack and air defense, by the mid-1970s the ground attack role was relinquished to the SEPECAT Jaguar. In 1987, seventy-five of the aircraft were fitted with new outer-wing panels manufactured by BAE, extending the life of the aircraft. However, in late 1992, just after their participation in the First Gulf War, flying out of RAF Aktori, Cyprus, British operation of the Phantom ceased.

Sea trials for many of the Royal Navy's Phantoms were conducted aboard USS Saratoga while operating in the Mediterranean. Here an 892 Squadron F-4K prepares to launch in May 1970.

Right: In the 1960s the Royal Air Force acquired the US-designated F-4M and RAF-designated Phantom FGR Mk. 2. This plane varied in several respects from the FG Mk. 1, including having a shorter nose strut. The FGR Mk. 2 was powered by two Rolls-Royce Spey 202/203 turbofan engines, and some of the other components of the plane were British built. Shown here is Phantom FGR Mk. 2, RAF serial number XT907. It carries an SUU-23/A 20 mm Vulcan gun pod on the centerline pylon. *National Museum of Naval Aviation*

The F-4N was the result of a USN program to rebuild and modernize 228 F-4Bs. Here, VF-111 F-4N BuNo. 151008 prepares to take off from USS *Franklin D. Roosevelt* (CV-42) in February 1977. *National Museum of Naval Aviation*

While Navy Phantom ranks had been heavily augmented with the production of the F-4J, some units continued to operate the F-4B, and by 1970 these aircraft were showing their age, and the wear of hard use. Accordingly, a reconditioning and modernization program was initiated, which was known as Bee Line, and 228 F-4Bs were processed through this program at NAS North Island, becoming F-4Ns.

After stripping and inspecting, the airframes were strengthened to combat fatigue. An F-4J-style slotted stabilator was installed, and the inboard leading-edge flaps were locked shut. Then, starting with an all-new wiring harness, the aircraft were rebuilt. New 30 kVA (kilovolt-ampere) constant-speed alternators were installed and new or rebuilt J79-GE-8 engines and other components were installed, as was a rebuilt radar suite.

Sanders AN/ALQ-126 or -126B deceptive electronic-countermeasures systems were installed, with the radar-homing/warning antenna mounted on the underside of the intakes and wings, aft of the landing-gear bays. The rebuilt aircraft were equipped with a helmet sight Visual Target Acquisition System (VTAS) and a Sidewinder Expanded Acquisition Mode (SEAM). Combat capability was further enhanced through the installation of a new dogfight mission computer and APX-76 or APX-80 IFF equipment. An AN/ASW-25 data link was installed, allowing automatic carrier landings.

The first flight of an F-4N occurred on June 4, 1972, with the first fleet deliveries taking place in February 1973.

Despite these improvements, and the considerable expense, the service life of the F-4N in the active Navy was relatively brief, and beginning in the mid-1970s the F-14 Tomcat began to supplant the Phantom in the fleet. The last active unit to turn in their F-4Ns was VF-154, which flew the type from USS *Coral Sea* until late 1983.

Both Navy and Marine Corps reserve units flew the F-4N a bit longer, with the last Navy F-4N being retired by VF-201 in February 1984, and VFMA-134 turning in the last of the type for the Marines the next year.

In addition to having many new structural parts, the F-4Ns had slotted stabilators like the F-4Js for better performance at low speeds and were equipped with DECM antennas on the engine-air intakes. Here, an F-4N of VF-21 lands on USS *Coral Sea* in 1981. *National Museum of Naval Aviation*

F-4N, BuNo 152293, of VF-111 "Sundowners" was photographed in a perfectly vertical attitude during a climb. The plane had a shark's mouth on the bottom of the nose, and the front and the rear of the centerline drop tank were painted red. *National Museum of Naval Aviation*

F-4B-19-MC 151491 was refurbished to an F-4N in the early 1970s and is seen here while assigned to VF-161 in the mid-1970s. *National Museum of Naval Aviation*

Another F-4B modernized to an F-4N was BuNo 153053, assigned to VF-84 "Jolly Rogers" and seen in an April 1974 photograph. The plane's modex, 201, is marked in black on the nose and on the yellow band at the top of the vertical tail. *National Museum of Naval Aviation*

In March 1975, an F-4N, BuNo 150415, speeds past Mount Etna in Sicily. This Phantom was assigned to VF-84, based on USS *Franklin D. Roosevelt* (CVA-42). On the tail is the skull-and-crossbones insignia of this squadron, nicknamed the "Jolly Rogers." *National Museum of Naval Aviation*

A TA-4J fitted as a small-scale tanker with a drogue and flexible hose attached to a centerline fuel tank is giving an in-air refueling to F-4N, BuNo 151406, of VF-201 around 1976. Another F-4N, BuNo 150435, flies in formation to the side. *National Museum of Naval Aviation*

On the runway at NAS Miramar in May 1977 is F-4N 152225, attached to VF-51, based on USS *Franklin D. Roosevelt*. The black object below the engine-air intake and above the tip of the centerline tank is an electronic-countermeasures antenna. *National Museum of Naval Aviation*

One aspect of Cold War gamesmanship was intercepting and escorting the opponent's warplanes. Such is the case with this F-4N from VF-111 that is accompanying a Soviet-built Tu-22 bomber over the Mediterranean. The bomber was being delivered to Libya in early 1977. *National Museum of Naval Aviation*

F-4N 152318 of VMFA-323 is a bolter, having failed to make an arrested landing on USS *Kitty Hawk* on February 19, 1979. The plane deployed its drag chute during the aborted landing, and the chute has just been jettisoned. The arrestor hook is still down. *National Museum of Naval Aviation*

During a flight out of NAS Fallon, Nevada, a Douglas KA-3B tanker refuels one of a group of Phantom IIs of VF-201 and VF-202 on June 11, 1979. The two closest Phantoms are F-4Ns, BuNos 153012 (*foreground*) and 152269. *National Museum of Naval Aviation*

The pilot of an F-4N of VMFA-531 is getting his footing on a step on the side of the fuselage as the plane is being towed into place on the flight deck of the carrier USS *Coral Sea* in the Indian Ocean in April 1980. A tow bar is attached to the nose gear. In the foreground is the cockpit of a Grumman A-6 Intruder-family aircraft. *National Museum of Naval Aviation*

Phantom IIs of VF-154 proceed over a snowy mountain range during an April 1981 flight out of NAS Fallon, Nevada. All four planes are F-4Ns. Their BuNos are, *from foreground to background*, 153027, 150419, 153053, and 152229. *National Museum of Naval Aviation*

An F-4N approaches USS *Coral Sea* for a landing during a cruise in the Indian Ocean on April 25, 1980. The plane was BuNo 152217 and was attached to VMFA-531 "Gray Ghosts." Armament consists of four Sidewinder air-to-air missiles. *National Museum of Naval Aviation*

F-4N 150482 of VF-201 "Hunters," a US Naval Reserve unit established in Dallas, is parked on USS *Saratoga* (CV-60) on February 23, 1983. From this angle, the slot to the immediate rear of the leading edge of the stabilator is clearly visible. *National Museum of Naval Aviation*

The F-4S program featured modernized and rebuilt F-4Js, of which several hundred were modified. Shown here is the first F-4S, BuNo 158360, still stenciled as an F-4J.

Just as the F-4Bs before them, by the mid-1970s the Navy F-4Js were showing their age, and an upgrade program intended to extend their life was launched, with the goal being to keep the aircraft serviceable until additional F-14s and the new F/A-18 became available.

The aircraft selected for this, constituting the F-4S program (and sources vary, giving 248 or 265 aircraft), were stripped and inspected. Structural improvements were made to the airframe, as well as to the landing gear. Straps, visible externally, were added to the wing spar to strengthen it. The hydraulic lines were replaced with new stainless-steel components, and a new wiring harness was installed on the aircraft.

To enhance maneuverability, a two-position wing leading-edge system was developed, which yielded a 50 percent improvement in turning ability during combat over unrebuilt aircraft. This system operated automatically as a function of the angle of attack but could be overridden by the pilot. Supply delays meant that the first forty-three F-4S aircraft were completed without them, but from November 1979 onward, all F-4S aircraft were equipped

with them as part of the rebuild process, and the two-section slats—one for the outboard part of the fixed inner wing and the other for the outer, folding, panel—were retrofitted to the first forty-three aircraft.

New engines, the so-called smokeless J79-GE-10B engines, were installed, aiding in concealment. A digital AWG-10B weapons control system was fitted, as were low-voltage formation lights.

The first flight of an F-4S was on July 22, 1977. The first unit equipped with the modernized aircraft was VMFA-451, which took delivery in June 1978. Like the F-4N, the carrier-borne service life of the F-4S was relatively brief.

In the East China Sea, at 9:12 a.m. on March 25, 1986, a VF-151 crew of Lt. Alan Colegrove, pilot, and Lt. Greg Blankenship, radar intercept officer (RIO), took off from USS *Midway* (CV-41) in Phantom 210, making the final carrier launch of a Phantom and closing a three-decade career. From then onward, Navy (and Marine) Phantoms served only with shore-based units, with VMFA-112 being the final unit to use the type, transitioning from the F-4S to the F/A-18A.

This VF-171 F-4S of the Key West Detachment was at Andrews Air Force Base, in August 1981. A major feature of the F-4S was two-position wing slats, which resulted in improved turning performance. The F-4S also was equipped with smokeless J79-GE-10B engines, which cut down on engine smoke that often could give away a plane's location to the enemy. The red, white, and blue shield on the side denotes that it is an Air Combat Maneuvering radar training aircraft. *Dana Bell*

F-4S 153885 of VF-301 "Devil's Disciples" appears in a photograph taken in about 1982. This squadron had acquired its F-4Ss two years earlier. Previously, this squadron had flown F-4Bs and F-4Ns. The "Devil's Disciples" were based at NAS Miramar. *National Museum of Naval Aviation*

An F-4S assigned to VF-301, based at NAS Miramar, cruises along the Southern California coast in 1982. The plane sports a three-tone-gray camouflage scheme on its upper and side surfaces and a low-visibility arrow device on the dorsal fin. *National Museum of Naval Aviation*

The pilot and the RIO of an F-4S attached to VF-301 prepare for a flight on USS *Constellation* (CV-64) off the coast of Southern California on June 28, 1982. A simplified inclined-V marking to indicate the danger zone for the engine-air intake is present. The "RESCUE" arrow to the front of that V has an interrupted black border around it.
National Museum of Naval Aviation

An F-4S assigned to VF-161 is viewed from a gallery along the flight deck of USS *Midway* (CV-41) on August 19, 1984. The plane is painted in a low-visibility camouflage scheme. The modex, 115, is marked on the nose-gear door and to the rear of the radome. *National Museum of Naval Aviation*

The same plane seen in the preceding photo is being rigged for a catapult launch on USS *Midway*. Each wing on the F-4S had an inboard slat extending from outboard of the inner pylon to the wing-fold joint, and an outboard slat from the wing-fold joint to the wingtip. *National Museum of Naval Aviation*

This colorful VF-202 F-4S was photographed at Naval Air Station Oceana on April 19, 1982. VF-202 was the last Navy tactical unit to fly the F-4S, transitioning to the F-14A in 1987. *Dana Bell*

F-4S 153908, with markings for VF-74 "Be-Devilers," based on USS *Forrestal*, is seen on the field at NAS Fallon on February 6, 1982. The aircraft has a low-visibility paint scheme but features a large national insignia in dark gray. *National Museum of Naval Aviation*

F-4S, BuNo 153483, is poised for a catapult launch on USS *Midway* in about 1984. Below the tail is the holdback cable, stretching from underneath the fuselage to the deck; this cable held the plane in place as it ramped up its engines just prior to launch. *National Museum of Naval Aviation*

In June 1984, an F-4S with markings for the Naval Air Test Center at Patuxent River, Maryland, drops a bomb over a test range. On the reddish-orange vertical fin are an insignia of the Naval Air Test Station and the tail code 7T in black letters shaded in white. *National Museum of Naval Aviation*

Two F-4S Phantom IIs of VF-301 soar over fog-enshrouded San Clemente Island off the Southern California coast on May 13, 1984. The closer plane was BuNo 155542, and the other one was 153874. Rearview mirrors are atop the rear canopies. *National Museum of Naval Aviation*

Lt. Cmdr. George "Black George" Kraus, executive officer of VF-202, puts his F-4S down on USS *America* (CV-66) on October 18, 1986, making the last operational landing of a Phantom aboard a carrier.

Two Phantoms of VMFA-212 rest on a tarmac at MCAS Kaneohe, Oahu, Hawaii, in April 1988. The nearest plane, F-4S BuNo 155805, has an ornate navy-blue-over-white paint job with Gothic lettering for the markings. *Steve Ginter*

Four F-4Js operated by the Blue Angels, the US Navy's elite precision-flying demonstration team, feature the Angels' signature navy blue with golden-yellow makings and trim. From 1969 to 1974 the Blue Angels flew F-4J Phantom IIs. The US Air Force's counterpart team, the Thunderbirds, also flew Phantom IIs at one point, making the Phantoms the only aircraft flown by both teams. *National Archives*

CHAPTER 8
USAF and the F-4C

That the F4H performance was impressive is undeniable. However, even that may have not been enough to persuade the Air Force to buy the aircraft were it not for Secretary of Defense Robert McNamara's insistence on increased commonalty among the service branches. While in some instances his mandate did not work out well, such as the F-111, in the case of the F-4, few would argue that this was not an excellent choice.

Following his edict, in 1961 the USAF began evaluating the F4H-1 Phantom II. The testing included a comparison with the Air Force F-106A, with the Phantom besting the Delta Dart in virtually every area.

To advance this program, in January 1962 the Navy loaned the Air Force F4H-1s with BuNos 149405 and 149406, which were repainted into USAF colors and for a time marked with serial numbers 62-1218 and 62-12169. Initial testing was done at Langley Air Force Base (AFB).

The Air Force was pleased with the results, and in March 1962 the Phantom was adopted as the standard tactical fighter and tactical reconnaissance aircraft of the USAF. On the thirtieth of the month, a letter of intent for one F-110A tactical fighter version, serial number 62-12199, was issued, and almost two months later a second letter was issued for a pair of RF-110A reconnaissance aircraft, serial numbers 62-12200 and 62-12201. The F-110 was to be known as the Spectre.

Specific Operational Requirement 200, issued by the Air Force on August 29, 1962, described an aircraft based on the F4H-1 but also equipped for ground attack. The aircraft was to retain the folding wings, catapult attachment points, and arrestor hooks of the F4H-1 but was to use larger, lower-pressure tires. The change in tires meant that the inner wing panels had to be bulged to make space. The aircraft was to be equipped with antiskid brakes.

However, the most notable difference from the Navy aircraft was that the rear cockpit was to be set up with flight controls for a second pilot.

The F-110 and RF-110A designations were short lived, since on September 18, 1962, aircraft designations were standardized across all services. Thus, the F-110 Spectre became the F-4 Phantom II. Suffix numbers would distinguish which branch of service the aircraft was manufactured for, with the F-110 becoming the F-4C.

On May 27, 1963, the first production F-4C (McDonnell Model 98DE), serial number 62-12199, clawed its way into the air for the first time, powered by two 10,000 lb.s.t. (17,000 lb.s.t. with afterburning) General Electric J79-GE-15 turbojets. It would be months before F-4Cs would reach USAF training units, and in the interim the Navy loaned the USAF twenty-seven more Phantoms, these being F-4Bs with BuNos 150480, 150486, 150493, 150630, 150634, 150643, 150649, 150650, 150652, 150653, 150994, 150995, 150997, 150999, 151000, 151002, 151004, 151006, 151007, 151009,151011, 151014, 151016, 151017, 151020, and 151021. The Air Force assigned the aircraft temporary serial numbers 62-12170 through 62-12196, and they were used by the 4453rd Combat Crew Training Wing at MacDill AFB in Florida pending arrival of the service's own F-4Cs.

In addition to the variations from the Navy F-4B, mentioned previously, the F-4C would use the USAF boom-type aerial-refueling gear, with a receptacle atop the fuselage aft of the rear cockpit rather than the Navy probe-and-drogue system.

The electronic suite of the F-4C was also much different from that of the F-4B, featuring a ground-mapping Westinghouse AN/APQ-100 radar system, a Litton AN/ASN-48 (LN12A/B) inertial navigation system, an AN/ASN-46 navigation computer, an ASN-39 (later -46) dead-reckoning navigation computer, a General Electric ASA-32A analog autopilot and flight-control system, an APN-141 (later -159) radar altimeter, and an A24G central air data computer. Offensive and defensive electronics included an AN/AJB-7 all-altitude nuclear bomb control system, an AN/APA-157 CW illuminator for the AIM-7 Sparrow air-to-air missiles, an ALR-

In 1969, the US Air Force Thunderbirds precision-flying exhibition team replaced its F-100s with F-4E Phantom IIs. The team flew these planes until 1974. The Thunderbird F-4Es were painted overall white, with red and blue trim. Here, a Thunderbird F-4E executes an upside-down flyover of an airfield with its landing gear extended. On the side of the engine intake are flags representing the countries the team had visited. *National Museum of the United States Air Force*

17 electronic-countermeasures radar-warning receiver, an APR-25 radar-homing/warning system, an APR-26 SAM launch-warning system, an ASQ-19 communications/navigation/ identification package, and an ARW-77 Bullpup missile control system.

While the F-4C had no built-in cannon armament, four AIM-7D or -7E Sparrow missiles could be carried in recesses underneath the fuselage, while four AIM-4D Falcon or AIM-9B or -9D Sidewinder infrared homing air-to-air missiles could be carried externally on the inboard underwing pylons.

In addition to the previously mentioned Bullpup, other air-to-ground missiles could be carried, including the AGM-45 Shrike and the AGM-65 Maverick, as well as unguided rocket launchers. The airframe could handle a maximum of 16,000 pounds of external stores. Following experiences in Vietnam, the F-4C were equipped to carry as many as three SUU-16/A (later -23/A) pods, each housing an M61A1 20 mm Vulcan cannon and 1,200 rounds of ammunition.

The 12th Tactical Fighter Wing became the first operational F-4C unit, beginning the transition from the F-84F in January 1964.

By the time F-4C production stopped on May 4, 1966, 583 examples had been produced.

The F-4C went to Southeast Asia in 1965, when the 15th Tactical Fighter Wing (TFW) deployed the 45th Tactical Fighter Squadron (TFS) to Thailand. On July 10 of that year, two F-4Cs used their Sidewinder missiles to down two MiG-17s over North Vietnam, making the first USAF kills of the Vietnam War. Conversely, the first US warplane to be shot down by a SAM was F-4C 63-7599 of the 47th Tactical Fighter Squadron, lost on July 24, 1965.

After two years over Vietnam, the USAF F-4C loss rate was dangerously close to 40 percent, pointing to the need for improvements. Trouble with the early air-to-air missiles, coupled with the lack of an internal gun, led to the installation of external gun pods, which seriously degraded aircraft performance, most notably in spin recovery. As a result, ejection was required if the spin was at less than 10,000 feet.

As the newer F-4D became available, the F-4Cs were transferred to Air Force National Guard and Reserve units beginning in 1972.

In January 1962, the US Air Force was authorized to procure a version of the McDonnell F4H-1 Phantom II under the designation F-110 Spectre. To commence this program, the Navy delivered two F4H-1s to the Air Force, including this one, BuNo 149406, which the US Air Force subsequently redesignated as USAF serial number 62-12169. This plane is shown with USAF markings but the USN BuNo. An array of armaments that the plane was capable of carrying are displayed in front of the aircraft. *National Museum of the United States Air Force*

The other F4H-1 Phantom II that the US Navy transferred to the US Air Force, BuNo 149405, redesignated F-110 Spectre, USAF serial number 62-12168, is seen in flight in USAF markings and tail number. On the fuselage is buzz number FJ-168. *National Museum of the United States Air Force*

This F4H-1 received from the Navy and assigned USAF serial number 62-12169 is seen during a flight out of Edwards AFB, California, on April 2, 1964. At the time the plane was test-firing two underwing SUU-16A gun pods. *National Museum of the United States Air Force*

The Air Force accepted the F-110 for production, redesignating it the F-4C in September 1962. The first production F-4C was rolled out in May 1963. Shown here is F-4C-20-MC, USAF serial number 63-7603. Two landing lights are recessed in the nose-gear door. *National Museum of the United States Air Force*

During a test flight from Edwards AFB on March 18, 1964, F-4C-15-MC 63-7410 carries two AGM-12 Bullpup air-to-ground missiles on the inboard pylons. The Bullpup was guided by a joystick control and was employed in the Vietnam War. *National Museum of the United States Air Force*

What better backdrop for a Phantom II based at Niagara Falls AFB than Niagara Falls? The plane is McDonnell F-4C-17-MC, USAF serial number 63-7523. The plane ended its career as a target at Aberdeen Proving Ground in the mid-1980s. *National Museum of the United States Air Force*

An F-4C approaches a tanker boom for refueling. Unlike the Navy Phantom IIs, which had pivoting probes for in-air refueling, the USAF Phantoms had a hydraulically actuated refueling receptacle on top of the fuselage, to the rear of the rear cockpit canopy. *National Museum of the United States Air Force*

In a photo of F-4C-15-MC 63-7407 at Eglin AFB, Florida, the extent of the stencils covering the fuselage and front nose-gear door is apparent. These include an arrow marked "RESCUE" for jettisoning the canopies, and black stripes above the steps. *National Museum of the United States Air Force*

Two Phantoms, with F-4C-15-MC 63-7408 in the foreground, are parked at an unidentified air base in October 1968. *National Museum of the United States Air Force*

In April 1963, a technician in McDonnell Aircraft overalls is loading a 2.75-inch folding-fin aerial rocket (FFAR) into an LAU-series nineteen-tube launcher, two of which are mounted on the inboard pylon of a Phantom. A seven-tube launcher also was available. *National Museum of the United States Air Force*

The Phantoms played a crucial role in the air war in Vietnam. Here, two F-4C-19-MCs take off from Da Nang Air Base (AB) in 1965. The one to the left, 63-7536, is in gray-and-white camouflage, while 63-7581 is in the camouflage developed for Southeast Asia. *National Museum of the United States Air Force*

F-4C-23-MC 64-0762 jettisons an SUU-7/A dispenser during a mission over mountainous terrain. An LAU-series multiple-rocket-launcher pod of a different, shorter model is secured to the inboard pylon. Such pods were used for ground-attack missions. *National Museum of the United States Air Force*

In the later summer of 1963, F-4C-18-MC, USAF serial number 73-0420, of the 310th Tactical Fighter Training Squadron, 58th Tactical Training Wing, flies over a mountainous desert area. The plane was based at Luke AFB, Arizona. *National Museum of the United States Air Force*

F-4C-22-MC 64-0673 was assigned to the 557th Tactical Fighter Squadron, 12th Tactical Fighter Wing, tail code XC, at Cam Ranh AB, South Vietnam, when this photo was taken of the plane making a chute-retarded landing on February 21, 1969. *National Museum of the United States Air Force*

McDonnell F-4C-24-MC 64-840 flies a high-altitude mission during 1966. The plane is painted in Southeast Asia camouflage, with a checkerboard pattern along the top of the vertical tail. *National Museum of the United States Air Force*

The nickname "Inferno" is stenciled on the air-conditioner intake of this F-4C fitted with an access ladder. The pilot's name, Capt. J. D. Allen, is marked on the canopy frame. On the engine intake is the insignia of the 433rd Tactical Fighter Squadron "Satan's Angels." *National Museum of the United States Air Force*

Bearing a Southeast Asia camouflage paint scheme, F-4C-22-MC 64-681 rests on a tarmac at Andersen AFB, Guam, on March 20, 1966. The tail number is marked on the vertical tail, but no squadron code is present on it. *National Museum of the United States Air Force*

F-4C-15-MC, USAF serial number 63-7411, was assigned to the 4457th Combat Crew Training Squadron, 4453rd Combat Crew Training Wing, when it was photographed at Davis-Monthan AFB, Arizona, on January 10, 1969. *National Museum of the United States Air Force*

F-4C-17-MC 63-7450 is parked on a tarmac at Davis-Monthan AFB, Tucson, Arizona, on January 10, 1969. This Phantom was assigned to the 4457th Combat Crew Training Squadron, based at Davis-Monthan from January 1964 to September 1971. *National Museum of the United States Air Force*

F-4C-23-MC 64-757 served with the 67th Tactical Fighter Squadron, based in East Asia from the late 1960s to the late 1970s. The squadron insignia on the fuselage features a fighting rooster in boxing gloves. *National Museum of the United States Air Force*

The same Phantom, F-4C-23-MC 64-0757, is viewed from the left side. The insignia on the left side of the fuselage is that of the 18th Tactical Fighter Wing. Although this plane technically was not a Wild Weasel, it was equipped for SAM-suppression missions. *National Museum of the United States Air Force*

F-4C-24-MC 64-0840 of the 414th Tactical Fighter Squadron, 57th Tactical Fighter Wing, based at Nellis AFB, wears that squadron's WD code on its tail in a May 1970 photograph. At the top of the tail is a yellow-and-black checkerboard. *National Museum of the United States Air Force*

The tail number of this Phantom, 37445, likely identifies the plane as F-4C-17-MC, USAF serial number 63-7445. The wavy, clearly defined demarcation between the upper gray and lower white camouflage colors are particularly apparent on this aircraft. *National Museum of the United States Air Force*

A ground crewman checks the right elevon of F-4C-24-MC 64-869, assigned to the Armament Development and Test Center (ADTC) at Eglin AFB, Florida, in 1972. The diamonds trim of the vertical tail was repeated on the drop tank. *National Museum of the United States Air Force*

F-4C-23-MC 64-0765 served with the 188th Tactical Fighter Group, Arkansas Air National Guard, and is seen in a photo taken around the 1980s. On the centerline pylon is a Vulcan 20 mm gun pod. A razorback insignia is on the engine intake. *National Museum of the United States Air Force*

CHAPTER 9
RF-4C

Virtually as soon as the decision was made that the US Air Force would fly what is now known as the Phantom, the branch desired a reconnaissance version. This is that aircraft, the YRF-110A preproduction test plane, which was later redesignated the YRF-4C. *National Archives*

The RF-4C (model 98DF) was the unarmed photoreconnaissance version of the F-4C. As noted in the previous chapter, work on the aircraft began under the designation RF-110A. Not surprisingly, this aircraft was similar to the Navy's RF-4B but was produced in much-higher numbers and, not surprisingly, was based on the USAF F-4C.

The first of the type, serial number 62-12200, by this time redesignated RF-4C, lifted off on its maiden flight on August 9, 1963. This aircraft had been converted from an F-4B. That first RF-4C aircraft featured the extended nose, indicative of the reconnaissance variants, but the camera gear was not actually installed. The second service test aircraft, serial number 62-12201, was equipped with the cameras, but little of the other specialized reconnaissance gear.

The RF-110A, like the F-110A, was redesignated on September 18, 1962, becoming the RF-4C. The production model of the aircraft first flew on May 18, 1964, and the type remained in production for almost ten years, with 503 examples having been produced when the last plane left the assembly line in December 1973.

During that time, the aircraft were equipped with an evolving array of cameras and other reconnaissance gear. Initially, the forward camera station (situated just behind the radar) carried a single forward oblique or vertical KS-87 camera, while the number 2 camera station (just behind the forward station) was fitted with either a KA-56 low-altitude camera or a vertical, left, and right oblique KS-87 camera. Station 3, the one just ahead of the cockpit, normally carried a single KA-55A or KA-91 high-altitude panoramic camera in a stabilized mount. For some flights, the high-altitude camera was replaced by two split vertical KS-87 cameras or KC-1 or T-11 mapping cameras. For night work, the RF-4C was equipped with a photoflash ejection system in the upper rear fuselage.

As built, the aircraft were equipped with Texas Instruments AN/APQ-99 two-lobe monopulse J-band radar, which in later service were replaced with Texas Instruments AN/APQ-172 sets.

On either side of the lower nose were the antennae for a Goodyear AN/APQ-102 side-looking mapping radar set.

The distinctive window for the reconnaissance camera is visible on the right nose of this 363rd Tactical Reconnaissance Wing RF-4C at it passes over a shoreline in 1980.

These aircraft could also carry the G-139 pod-mounted General Dynamics HIAC-1 LOROP (LOng-Range Oblique Photography) camera system on the fuselage centerline. This camera could capture detailed images from as far as 100 miles away and was often used along North Korean and eastern European borders. Not surprisingly, the underslung gear markedly degraded the Phantom's performance. To overcome this, twenty-four RF-4Cs were modified to carry a CAI KS-127A or KS-127F LOROP camera with a 66-inch focal length in camera stations 2 and 3.

Twenty RF-4Cs were modified in 1970 to incorporate the ARN-92 LORAN-D navigation system, giving the aircraft all-weather capability.

Initially, the RF-4C was not equipped to carry any weapons but for emergency provision to carry a nuclear weapon on the centerline station. However, before the type was retired, the RF-4Cs were modified so that AIM-9 Sidewinders could be carried on the inner underwing pylons.

The 16th Tactical Reconnaissance Squadron (TRS) of the 363rd Tactical Reconnaissance Wing (TRW) at Shaw AFB was the first operational unit to be equipped with the RF-4C. This squadron was deployed to Tan Sun Nhut in South Vietnam in October 1965. In February 1967, the 15th TRS also deployed to Southeast Asia.

Field use of the RF-4C made apparent a number of problems and deficiencies, including, notably, the reliability of the AN/APQ-102A side-looking radar, some of which took years to correct. From their arrival until 1972, the RF-4Cs were used in day missions all over Vietnam and Laos, typically flying without escort. Despite this, none were lost to MiGs, but seven were shot down by SAMs and a further sixty-five were lost to AAA or small arms. A further four were destroyed on the ground, and seven in operational mishaps. While at a glance the loss rate seems high, given the number of sorties and seven years in theater, it was not exceptional.

The long, horizontal lever to the left side of the instrument panel of the YRF-4C is the landing-gear control handle. To the rear of the instrument panel is the pilot's control stick. The radarscope at the top of the instrument panel is clearly visible. *National Museum of the United States Air Force*

In this view of the front instrument panel of the YRF-4C preproduction test plane, a radarscope is present at the top of the panel, but the mapping and reconnaissance viewfinder, which was to the right of the radarscope on the RF-4C, is not present. *National Museum of the United States Air Force*

The rear instrument panel of the YRF-4C was almost pure F-4B. On the right side of the upper panel of the instrument panel are inertial navigation controls. On the left side of the upper panel are various light switches. Along the bottom of the panel are flight gauges. *National Museum of the United States Air Force*

The rear cockpit of the YRF-4C had more in common with the F-4B, from which it was converted, than the production RF-4C, although this cockpit did have a control stick, given the Air Force's inclusion of flight controls in its Phantoms' rear cockpits. *National Museum of the United States Air Force*

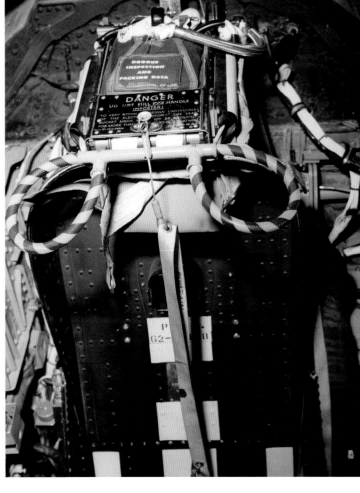

The pilot's Martin-Baker ejection seat in the YRF-4C is seen from above. A sticker on the seat includes this plane's USAF serial number, 62-12168. The parachute pack, which served as a seat back, and the seat bottom, which contained a survival pack, are not installed. *National Museum of the United States Air Force*

The pilot's Martin-Baker ejection seat from YRF-4C 62-12168 is seen from a closer perspective. The two loops with the two-colored stripes are handles for pulling down a face curtain prior to ejection. At the top rear of the seat is the top of the drogue parachute. *National Museum of the United States Air Force*

RF-4C-20-MC, USAF serial number 64-1001, is seen from a tanker with its refueling receptacle deployed. The McDonnell RF-4C was an unarmed version of the F-4C, with a redesigned nose that contained photoreconnaissance equipment and a smaller radar antenna than that of the F-4C. The RF-4C also carried infrared imaging equipment for use in reconnaissance. *National Museum of the United States Air Force*

Personnel survey the damages in the aftermath of a nose-gear failure on McDonnell RF-4C-23-MC, USAF serial number 64-1076. At the rear of the fuselage, the tail cone, which served as a door for the drag chute, is in the open position. *National Museum of the United States Air Force*

One of the earliest RF-4Cs, USAF serial number 63-7742, is parked inside an aircraft shelter, wings folded. "ALL WEATHER" is painted in red on the fuselage, aft of the rear cockpit. The buzz number FJ-742 is in black on the side of the fuselage. *National Museum of the United States Air Force*

Phantoms were equipped with a drag chute in the tail of the fuselage to enable them to use shorter runways, and this RF-4C has just deployed its chute while landing at Gulfport AFB, Mississippi, during Exercise Photo Finish 81 in October 1981. *National Museum of the United States Air Force*

RF-4C-31-MC, USAF serial number 66-0435, is seen while serving with the California National Guard. A red-colored cover is over the engine intake. Though not very visible, to the immediate rear of the air-conditioning scoop was a radar-mapping radome. *National Museum of the United States Air Force*

The first plane of the RF-4C-20-MC production block was this Phantom, USAF serial number 64-0997, seen in California National Guard markings. This plane has a late-style, slightly rounded chin, as opposed to the flatter, early-type chin. *National Museum of the United States Air Force*

McDonnell RF-4C-28-MC 65-0942 is in markings for the California Air National Guard. To the front of the air-conditioner scoop is the window for the left low-altitude camera. A forward camera is pointed down through a window at the front of the camera bulge. *National Museum of the United States Air Force*

Specifically configured to meet the needs of the Tactical Air Command (TAC), the F-4D would be the mount flown by three of the Air Force's aces in Vietnam.

Authorized in March 1964, the type first flew on Pearl Harbor Day 1965. Series deliveries began in March 1966. Externally, the F-4D is difficult to discern from its predecessor, and it used the same engines, but the avionics of the D were vastly superior.

Inside the radome was an AN/APA-165 radar set. Built around the partially solid-state AN/APQ-109A, the -163 introduced an air-to-ground ranging mode using movable cursors. Other electronic systems also were updated with smaller, lighter, better components, including the ASN-63 inertial navigation system and Collins ASQ-19 miniaturized communication/navigation/identification suite.

The F-4D was equipped with an AN/ASQ-91 weapons release computer system. This system combined radar data concerning the slant range to the target with aircraft speed, attitude, and climbing rate, to release the bomb at the proper point. To facilitate the delivery of laser-guided bombs, an AJB-7 all-altitude bomb delivery system connected to an ASQ-91 weapons release computer was provided. Frequently, a CRT display was provided in the back seat, which was linked to the bomb-homing system.

The centerline pylon was equipped with a multiple ejector rack, and the inboard underwing pylons with triple ejector racks.

The Sidewinder capability of the inboard underwing pylon F-4C was discarded in favor of the Hughes AIM-4D Falcon infrared-homing missile. In service, the Falcon did not fare well, and as a result the aircraft were modified to restore the Sidewinder capability.

Missile sighting was accomplished through an AN/ASG-22 lead computing optical sight with amplifier and gyro.

F-4Ds began to replace F-4Cs in the skies over Vietnam in the spring of 1967, and the first MiG kill by an F-4D was on June 5 of that year, when two crewmen, Maj. Everett T. Raspberry and Capt. Francis Gullick, shot down a MiG-17 near Hanoi. Ultimately, the type was credited with destroying forty-five enemy aircraft.

During 1968–69, the Combat Tree modification was begun. This program allowed the retention of a full missile load while carrying electronic-countermeasures gear. To do so, an attachment point for a countermeasures pod was added to the inboard pylon, which could then also carry two more AIM-9J Sidewinder missiles on each side.

The F-4D was also exported, with the Nirou Havai Shahanshahiye Iran (Imperial Iranian Air Force) ordering thirty-two newly built aircraft under the Shah of Iran in 1967, and the Republic of Korea purchasing forty-two examples, those being USAF surplus rather than new builds. With the overthrow of the Shah in 1979, shipments of replacement parts to Iran were embargoed. Despite this, through local manufacturing and illicit procurement of parts, the country has managed to keep the F-4Ds (and Es) flying into the twenty-first century.

In the late 1970s, the USAF began to transfer the F-4Ds to Air Guard and Reserve units, with others being sent for storage and reclamation. By the late 1980s, all had been withdrawn from service.

The McDonnell F-4D was the first model of Phantom built entirely to USAF specifications, on the basis of the F-4C airframe but including improved air-to-air and air-to-ground attack capabilities. It featured the infrared sensor under the nose, with the extra bulge toward its lower rear. Seen here is F-4D-30-MC, serial number 66-7554. This Phantom still exists and has been on display at the Museum of Aviation, Warner Robbins AFB, Georgia. *National Museum of the United States Air Force*

Phantom engines could be started by an external pneumatic source (a "start cart") or by firing blank cartridges. This photo shows a cartridge start, which generated a mass of black smoke. The plane is F-4D-29-MC 66-269 of the 417th Tactical Fighter Squadron. *National Museum of the United States Air Force*

A tractor with a tow bar is maneuvering an F-4D with a load of bombs and Sparrow missiles in front of a hardened aircraft shelter at Da Nang AB on February 16, 1971. The plane was assigned to the 390th Tactical Fighter Squadron, 366th Tactical Fighter Wing. *National Museum of the United States Air Force*

"Bobbie II" is marked on the air-conditioner scoop of F-4D-31-MC 66-7750 of the 433rd Tactical Fighter Squadron, 8th Tactical Fighter Wing, Ubon Royal Thai AFB, in 1968. The star indicates a MiG kill by Capt. William Kirk and 1Lt. Theodore Bongartz. *National Museum of the United States Air Force*

The "FP" code on this Phantom pertained to the 497th Tactical Fighter Squadron, 8th Tactical Fighter Wing, Ubon Royal Thai AFB. The 500-pound bombs are fitted with "daisy-cutter" fuse extensions, for detonating the bombs above the ground. *National Museum of the United States Air Force*

An F-4D of the 433rd Tactical Fighter Squadron, 8th Tactical Fighter Wing, deploys its drag chute as it lands at an airfield. During the Vietnam War, this squadron used the FG tail code and was based at Ubon Royal Thai AFB in Thailand. *National Museum of the United States Air Force*

F-4D-28-MC 65-0724 of the 435th Tactical Fighter Squadron, 8th Tactical Fighter Squadron, is manned and on a tarmac, probably after a mission, judging from the empty weapons pylons. The refueling receptacle is in the raised position atop the fuselage. *National Museum of the United States Air Force*

A Phantom II assigned to the 497th Tactical Fighter Squadron, 8th Tactical Fighter Wing, Ubon Royal Thai AFB, is parked in a revetment. The tail number, 68/802, probably pertains to USAF serial number 66-8802, which was an F-4D-33-MC. The 500-pound bombs on the inboard pylon have "daisy-cutter" fuse extensions. A LORAN "towel rack" dorsal antenna, part of the LORAN precision navigation system, is mounted on the aircraft. *National Museum of the United States Air Force*

An F-4D of the 389th Tactical Fighter Squadron, 366th Tactical Fighter Wing, based at Da Nang, South Vietnam, unleashes a volley of 2.75-inch FFARs on an enemy concentration. Each aircraft of this squadron had a different letter following the A in the tail code; this one is AY. *National Museum of the United States Air Force*

Engines running, F-4D-26-MC 64-0979 of the 8th Tactical Fighter Squadron, 49th Tactical Fighter Wing, pauses on a hardstand at Elmendorf AFB, Alaska, on August 7, 1969. The tail code is HC. The wing-mounted drop tank is painted in at least two colors. *National Museum of the United States Air Force*

An F-4D of the 8th Tactical Fighter Squadron, 49th Tactical Fighter Wing, is parked on a tarmac at Elmendorf AFB, Alaska, on August 7, 1969. Typical USAF practice at the time was to mark the last three digits of the serial number on the nose-gear door. *National Museum of the United States Air Force*

F-4D-30-MC 66-7617 of the 4533rd Tactical Training Squadron, 33rd Tactical Fighter Wing, Eglin AFB, Florida, is seen on May 5, 1970. It is carrying a QRC-335-3 pod: quick-reaction-capability version of the ALQ-101 ECM pod. *National Museum of the United States Air Force*

F-4D-28-MC 65-0720 of the 555th Tactical Fighter Squadron, 432nd Tactical Fighter Wing, based at Udorn Royal Thai AFB, was photographed at Phù Cát AB, in Bình Định Province, South Vietnam, on September 19, 1970. *National Museum of the United States Air Force*

McDonnell F-4D-25-MC 64-0951 wears the tail code HD, indicating it was assigned to the 9th Tactical Fighter Squadron, 49th Tactical Fighter Wing, dually based at Holloman AFB, New Mexico, and Spangdahlem AB in the Federal Republic of Germany. This photograph was taken prior to 1972, because in that year all the squadrons of the 49th TFW standardized their tail codes as HO. *National Museum of the United States Air Force*

An ECM pod is mounted under the forward left Sparrow missile bay on F-4D-30-MC 66-7609 of the 432nd Tactical Reconnaissance Fighter Wing as it makes a drag-chute retarded landing at Udorn Royal Thai AFB, October 1972. *National Museum of the United States Air Force*

Laser-guided smart bombs are on the wing pylons of F-4D-26-MC 66-0234 of the 435th Tactical Fighter Squadron, 8th Tactical Fighter Wing, based at Ubon Royal Thai AFB, as it proceeds on a mission to North Vietnam in September 1972. *National Museum of the United States Air Force*

F-4D-31-MC 66-7688 served with the 90th Tactical Fighter Squadron, 405th Tactical Fighter Wing, with the home base of Clark AFB, Republic of the Philippines. Below the windscreen is the squadron's "Pair-O-Dice" insignia. *National Museum of the United States Air Force*

Landing gear and flaps extended, F4D-30-MC 66-7549 of the 22nd Tactical Fighter Squadron, 36th Tactical Fighter Wing, comes in for a landing at Spangdahlem AB, West Germany, in May 1971. This squadron was based at Bitburg. *National Museum of the United States Air Force*

An F-4D is parked inside an aircraft shelter. Aircraft shelters could be simple metal covers, or a layer of concrete could be added to the outside of them to form a hardened aircraft shelter capable of protecting a parked plane from enemy attack. *National Museum of the United States Air Force*

This F-4D-28-MC, USAF serial number 65-0724, is equipped for close support, with FFAR launcher pods on the inboard pylons and a Vulcan 20 mm gun pod on the centerline pylon. The plane was attached to the 435th Tactical Fighter Squadron. *National Museum of the United States Air Force*

F-4D-26-MC, USAF serial number 65-0589, is being prepared for a bombing mission, with 500-pound bombs shackled to the pylons. The infrared sensors under the noses of the F-4Ds had a bulge on the lower rear that was not present on the sensors on F-4Cs. *National Museum of the United States Air Force*

F-4D-30-MC, USAF serial number 66-7551, of the 482nd Tactical Fighter Wing at Homestead AFB, Florida, is armed with a Maverick AGM-65 air-to-ground precision guided missile on the left rail of the right inboard pylon. *National Museum of the United States Air Force*

In the years before the Iranian Revolution in 1979, the United States transferred a total of thirty-two F-4Ds to the Imperial Iranian Air Force. Among those aircraft was this example—here armed with a Vulcan pod—an F-4D-35-MC numbered 3-602 on the tail, formerly USAF serial number 67-14870. *National Museum of the United States Air Force*

This F-4D of the 113th Tactical Fighter Wing, 121st Tactical Fighter Squadron, makes a pass over an air base on March 10, 1989, near the end of its service life. *Dana Bell*

CHAPTER 11

F-4E: The Return of the Gunfighter

Back in 1954, when initial design work on what would become the Phantom began, it was proposed to arm the aircraft with four 20 mm cannons. However, the jet-age thinking of the military at that time was that guns were essentially obsolete, and missile armament would be the wave of the future.

Thus, each of the Phantoms was armed with missiles (and bombs)—until the F-4E—the return of the gunfighter.

Air combat over Vietnam showed not only that missiles were much more expensive than ammunition, but that they oftentimes were also notably unreliable. Even before the smoke of J79s filled the skies of Southeast Asia, McDonnell had again proposed a cannon-armed Phantom, with the company in March 1961 proposing that the M61 Vulcan be mounted inside the aircraft—a notion that the government dismissed.

Again in 1964 the company proposed such a configuration, this time getting funding to create this in June 1965. In order to fit the large weapon inside the already cramped Phantom airframe, it was proposed that the long nose of the RF-4C be adapted. Inside the nose was an AN/APG-30 radar set, and just beneath it in a pod was a 20 mm General Electric M61A1 rotary six-barrel cannon.

To test the new configuration, YRF-4C 62-12200 was modified, becoming the YF-4E. Flying for the first time on August 7, 1965, the aircraft was equipped with a gunsight scavenged from an F-100D.

Encouraged by the results of those test flights, two more YF-4Es were authorized and were converted from F-4C (63-7445) and F-4D (65-0713). Installing the Vulcan in the nose required a new ammunition feed system be developed, and its proximity to the radar set meant that highly effective and reliable vibration dampers and noise/blast eliminators had to be engineered.

After further testing, in August 1966, ninety-six F-4Es were ordered. The first production example took to the air on June 30, 1967.

Because of the forward position of the heavy gun and its 639-round ammunition drum, in order to maintain balance a 95-gallon fuel tank was installed in the rear fuselage, which brought the internal capacity to 1,993 gallons. The big gun also meant that a small radar set had to be used, in the form of the solid-state Westinghouse AN/APQ-120 X-band radar unit.

While gaining the much-needed internal gun, the F-4E retained the AIM-7 Sparrow air-to-air missile mounts and the external store stations of the earlier models. Weight was increasingly a consideration, so the powered folding-wing mechanism found on all prior Phantoms was eliminated, as was the emergency ram-air turbine previously housed inside a recess on the upper rear fuselage. In time, the elimination of the turbine proved a mistake.

The F-4E was powered by a pair of J79-GE-17 engines with an afterburning thrust of 17,900 pounds. Beginning with the second production F-4E, BuNo 66-0285, the aircraft were fitted with a slotted stabilator, which helped offset the increased weight of the nose by increasing tailplane effectiveness. At the same time, the long "turkey feather" afterburner was added.

During the course of production, self-sealing fuel tanks began to be installed rather than the earlier bladders, a change that reduced fuel capacity by 140 gallons.

Other notable changes made during the course of F-4E production included the use of thicker lower wing skins, allowing the elimination of the steel reinforcing strap, and the incorporation of leading-edge wing slats. The latter greatly enhanced maneuverability. So successful was this that the USAF retrofitted these to previously produced F-4Es as well.

At production block 53, J79-GE-17C or -17E engines with low-smoke combustors began to be used, making the Phantom less readily visible to enemy gunners. At about the same time, the Phantom's gun installation was upgraded through the installation of long blast diffusers to the barrels. This not only made the gun quieter, increasing the chance of surprising the enemy, but, more notably, partially eliminated the earlier prior tendency of the engines to ingest gun gases, which caused flameouts. This problem had been initially addressed at block 48 through the installation of a "derichment system." This system was actuated when the gun-firing circuit closed, and it enabled either engine to dump gun-gas-enriched air before it could enter the engine compressor and cause a flameout. This improvement was retrofitted to earlier F-4Es as well.

F-4Es began to be deployed to Southeast Asia in November 1968. Ultimately, nine squadrons were deployed, and the F-4Es were credited with twenty-one MiG kills during the war. Of these, ten were brought down by Sparrows, five with gunfire, four with Sidewinders, one with a combination of Sidewinder and gunfire, and one without any use of weapons.

Unarmed F-4Es were flown by the USAF Thunderbirds flight demonstration team from June 1969 until 1974, when the desire for greater fuel economy caused the team to transition to the T-38 Talon trainer.

In 1975, USAF combat units began transitioning to the F-15 Eagle, with the F-4Es being retired from combat units in 1989–90.

McDonnell Douglas produced 1,387 F-4Es over twelve years, more—and over a longer period—than any other variant. Of these, 993 were for the USAF, and 394 for Foreign Military Sales (FMS). The last F-4E, built for Korea, rolled off the end of the production line on October 25, 1979.

A further 138 F-4EJ aircraft were built by Mitsubishi in Japan, where production continued until May 20, 1981. Of the all-time total of 5,057 McDonnell Douglas–built Phantom IIs, 1,264 were for Navy and Marine Corps use and 2,874 were for the USAF, and the rest went to foreign customers.

F-4E Specifications	
Type	two-seat fighter-bomber
Crew	two, pilot and weapons system operator
Length	63 feet
Height	16 feet, 5 inches
Span	38 feet, 4 inches
Engines	2 General Electric J79-GE-17s at 17,900 pounds thrust in afterburner
Empty weight	29,535 pounds
Combat weight	41,135 pounds
Maximum takeoff weight	58,000 pounds
Maximum speed	Mach 2.24
Rate of climb	41,300 feet/minute
Combat ceiling	57,200 feet
Total internal fuel	2,056 gallons
Combat radius	367 miles
Ferry range	1,400 nautical miles
Armament	one M61A-1 20 mm Gatling cannon with 639 rounds
	four AIM-7 Sparrow radar-guided missiles
	four AIM-9 Sidewinder heat-seeking missiles
	two 370-gallon underwing fuel tanks
	one 600-gallon centerline fuel tank
	various ordnance packages
Number built	969

The McDonnell F-4E was developed to give the Phantom an aerial-gunnery capability in addition to its air-to-air missiles, which sometimes proved ineffective in aerial combat. The gun was to be housed inside a chin fairing, as seen in this photo of one of three preproduction test aircraft, YF-4E 65-0713. Under the belly of the plane is an A/A47U-3A tow target system, consisting of an RMK-19 reeling-machine launcher with a propeller on the front, and, *below it*, a red-colored towable target. *National Museum of the United States Air Force*

McDonnell YF-4E 65-0713 executes a bank over a desert test range, revealing more of the shape of the fairing for the gun, the M61A1 20 mm rotary cannon. The forward door of the nose landing gear included the rear part of the gun fairing. *National Museum of the United States Air Force*

When this photograph was taken, YF-4E 65-0713 was being used to test a rudder made of boron fiber, a lightweight, high-strength material that now sees widespread use in the aerospace industry. The plane carries AGM-65 Maverick guided air-to-ground missiles. *National Museum of the United States Air Force*

"BORON" is written on the rudder of YF-4E 65-0713. A shorter muzzle cover is on the gun fairing than in the preceding photo. Also, during its career, this plane was used to test the concept of an F-4-based Wild Weasel, which would culminate in the F-4G. *National Museum of the United States Air Force*

Several Phantoms were converted to YF-4Es to test the feasibility of mounting a 20 mm rotary cannon under the nose of the aircraft. This one started out as F-4C-17-MC 63-7445 and is seen during a flight test during March 1967. *National Museum of the United States Air Force*

The F-4E's gun, the M61A1 20 mm rotary cannon, was mounted in a fairing or gondola below the nose and the front of the fuselage. It had a rate of fire of 6,000 rounds per minute and was supplied with 639 rounds of ammunition. Shown here is F-4E-32-MC 66-0323 along with an array of some of the missiles it could carry. To the front on a stand is an M61A1 cannon, with the ammunition drum above it. *National Museum of the United States Air Force*

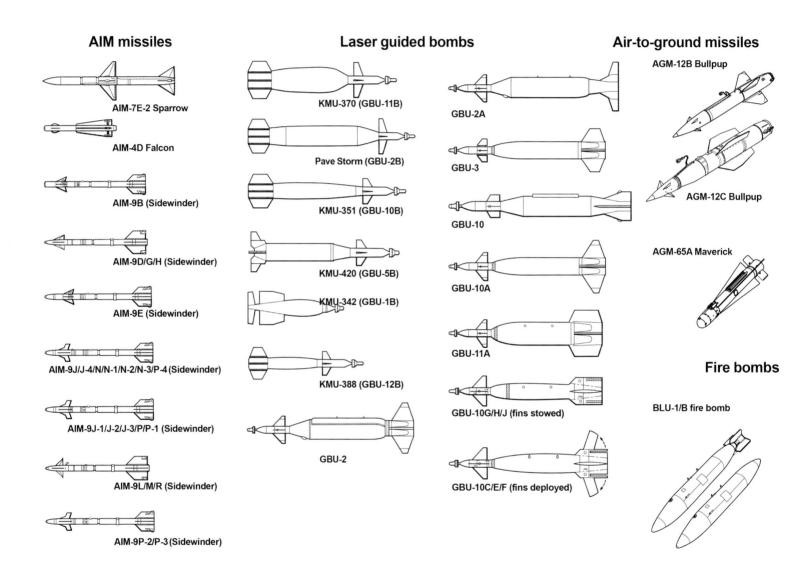

AIM missiles

AIM-7E-2 Sparrow

AIM-4D Falcon

AIM-9B (Sidewinder)

AIM-9D/G/H (Sidewinder)

AIM-9E (Sidewinder)

AIM-9J/J-4/N/N-1/N-2/N-3/P-4 (Sidewinder)

AIM-9J-1/J-2/J-3/P/P-1 (Sidewinder)

AIM-9L/M/R (Sidewinder)

AIM-9P-2/P-3 (Sidewinder)

Laser guided bombs

KMU-370 (GBU-11B)

Pave Storm (GBU-2B)

KMU-351 (GBU-10B)

KMU-420 (GBU-5B)

KMU-342 (GBU-1B)

KMU-388 (GBU-12B)

GBU-2

GBU-2A

GBU-3

GBU-10

GBU-10A

GBU-11A

GBU-10G/H/J (fins stowed)

GBU-10C/E/F (fins deployed)

Air-to-ground missiles

AGM-12B Bullpup

AGM-12C Bullpup

AGM-65A Maverick

Fire bombs

BLU-1/B fire bomb

The F-4E could be armed with these external stores.

A quartet of four 500-pound "dumb" bombs fall away from F-4E-38-MC, USAF serial number 67-347, of the 347th Tactical Fighter Wing, from Moody AFB, Georgia. A laser-guided smart bomb and a Pave Spike laser designator are mounted under the plane.

F-4E-32-MC Phantom II, serial number 66-0330, serves with the 57th Fighter-Interceptor Squadron (FIS), based at Keflavík, in southwestern Iceland, in 1970. To counterbalance the weight of the nose-mounted M61A1 20 mm cannon with its 639-round drum magazine, a 95-gallon fuel tank was added in the rear fuselage, increasing internal fuel capacity to 1,993 gallons.

F-4E-62-MC 74-1640 and F-4E-59-MC 73-1189 of the 4th Tactical Fighter Wing are parked at Luke AFB, Arizona, in July 1983. The third plane is F-4C-23-MC 64-0776, which scored three MiG kills over Vietnam in 1967.
National Museum of the United States Air Force

F-4E, flown by Capt. Tom Gibbs, Thunderbirds Slot, has the blackened tail from flying in the exhaust of Thunderbirds Lead.

This 347 Tactical Fighter Wing F-4E shows off the array of stores that the type could carry.

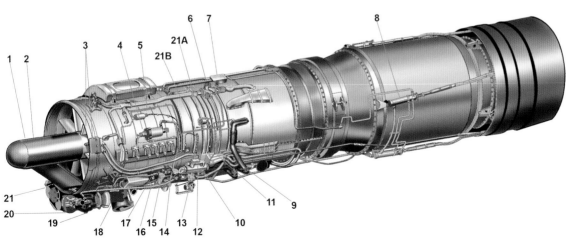

No.	Item
1	AC generator
2	Constant speed drive unit
3	Air/oil cooler and valve
4	Anti-icing indicator switch
5	Variable vane actuator
6	Anti-icing valve
7	Heat shield
8	Nozzle actuator
9	Compressor bleed air manifold
10	Nozzle area control
11	Oil pressure transmitter
12	Afterburner oil cooler
13	Torque booster
14	Afterburner ignition switch
15	Scavenge oil filter
16	Afterburner fuel control
17	Afterburner fuel filter
18	Temperature amplifier
19	Afterburner fuel pump
20	Control alternator
21	Compressor inlet temperature sensor
21A	* CDP switch
21B	* T5 reset cutout switch
	* J-79-17 engine only

They are smiling now, but the crew of F-4E-35-MC, USAF serial number 67-0321, of the 421st Tactical Fighter Squadron doubtless were not so happy when the tail of their Phantom was shot up over Vietnam. The scene was the Da Nang AB in 1973. *National Museum of the United States Air Force*

F-4E-32-MC 66-324 is being readied for its next flight at George AFB, Victorville, California, in July 1969. At the time, this Phantom was serving with the 431st Tactical Fighter Squadron, 479th Tactical Fighter Wing, at George AFB. *National Museum of the United States Air Force*

McDonnell F-4E-41-MC, USAF serial number 68-0526, of the 526th Tactical Fighter Squadron, 26th Tactical Reconnaissance Wing, based at Ramstein AB, West Germany, visits a British airfield in June 1971. *National Museum of the United States Air Force*

McDonnell F-4E-32-MC, USAF serial number 66-333, of the 336th Tactical Fighter Squadron, 4th Tactical Fighter Wing, was photographed at Seymour Johnson AFB, North Carolina, in 1971. The 4th TFW's insignia is on the fuselage. *National Museum of the United States Air Force*

Two USAF technicians adjust an AN/ALQ-171(V) pod, designed to jam enemy radio transmissions. It is mounted on F-4E-58-MC, serial number 73-01187. Pale-yellow formation lights called tape lights are to the front of the intake and on the fuselage. *National Museum of the United States Air Force*

Ground crewmen at Seymour Johnson AFB service a 225th Fighter Squadron F-4E in December 1989. *Dana Bell*

F-4E-34-MC 67-0247 of the 4th Tactical Fighter Squadron, 33rd Tactical Fighter Wing, based at Eglin AFB, exhibits the early type of short muzzle cover at the front of the gun fairing. The cover was black, and the top of it fitted snugly to the fuselage. *National Museum of the United States Air Force*

At William Tell '76, a biennial aerial-gunnery competition, an F-4E is parked near a group of Lockheed T-33 trainers. On the underside of the wing, to the front of the drop tank, are the three actuator fairings associated with the wing slat to their front. *National Museum of the United States Air Force*

The "FD" squadron code is on the tail of this F-4E-33-MC, USAF serial number 66-0351, of the 45th Tactical Fighter Squadron, 15th Tactical Fighter Wing, based at MacDill AFB, Florida, during a flight over Mount McKinley, Alaska, on August 29, 1979. *National Museum of the United States Air Force*

Ground crewmen clear snow from the wing of F-4E-36-MC, USAF serial number 66-0368. A tape light is visible on the side of the fuselage, to the front of the man to the right, and a diagonally oriented tape light is present on the vertical fin. *National Museum of the United States Air Force*

An F-4E makes a vertical climb in a January 1981 photograph. The plane was assigned to the 51st Fighter Wing, based at Osan AB, South Korea. On the tail is the "OS" code, particular to the 51st Fighter Wing. An ECM pod is mounted under the fuselage. *National Museum of the United States Air Force*

In this remarkable view, an F-4E Phantom II is coupled to the refueling boom of a tanker. The Phantom lacks wing pylons, and no missiles are mounted. On the bottom of the fairing for the Vulcan 20 mm rotary cannon, several sets of ventilation louvers are visible. *National Museum of the United States Air Force*

A 347th Tactical Fighter Wing F-4E releases a pair of bombs on a target. Although the tail number is very obscure, it is 68318, which translates to USAF serial number 68-318, which was that of an F-4E-37-MC. *National Museum of the United States Air Force*

An F-4E-59-MC, USAF serial 73-01203, of the 3rd Tactical Fighter Wing, staging out of Misawa AB, Japan, flies a mission during Exercise Cope North '80. This exercise helped develop cooperation between military forces of Pacific Basin allies. *National Museum of the United States Air Force*

A former Egyptian air force F-4E after reassignment to the 52nd Tactical Fighter Wing at Spangdahlem AB, West Germany. This aircraft still carries the yellow-and-black identification markings that the Egyptian air force applied to differentiate their F-4s from those operated by the Israeli air force.

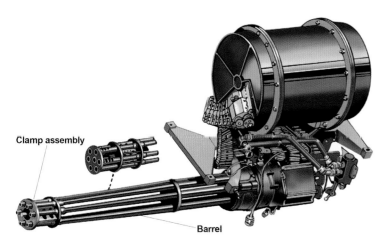

Clamp assembly

Barrel

The General Electric M61A1 consists of a housing that encloses and supports a rotating assembly. Each of the six barrels fires a single 20 mm round per revolution, which enables a high rate of fire with little danger of overheating. It is air cooled, externally driven, and normally fuselage or pod mounted.

The F-4 Phantom was equipped with the Mk. 7 Martin Baker ejection seat.

This protrusion on the leading edge of the left wing of the F-4E is a new feature that houses the Northrop ASX-1 Target Identification System Electro-Optical (TISEO). A long-range electro-optical sensor, TISEO provided imaging of targets beyond visual range. *National Museum of the United States Air Force*

An F-4E flies, landing gear lowered, over an air base in the desert. The only visible identification markings are on the vertical tail: "USAF" over the tail number, 60966. Yellow tape lights are on the tail, on the center of the fuselage, and below the cockpit. *National Museum of the United States Air Force*

F-4E-39-MC 68-0449 still had markings for the 457th Tactical Fighter Squadron, 301st Tactical Fighter Wing, when photographed at Tracor Flight Systems, Mojave, California, in 1993. The plane was about to be converted to a QF-4E remote-controlled aerial target. *National Museum of the United States Air Force*

US Air Force serial number 62-12200, originally a YRF-4C and later converted to a YF-4E, went on to serve as the test bed for two small canard wings, as seen here. These canards were installed to test the Precision Aircraft Control Technology (PACT). *National Museum of the United States Air Force*

F-4E-37-MC 68-0338 of the 131st Tactical Fighter Wing, Missouri Air National Guard, flies over the Missouri state capitol in Jefferson City during 1988. The plane, which was a two-time MiG killer, was marked to commemorate thirty years of "Phabulous Phantoms." *National Museum of the United States Air Force*

CHAPTER 12
F-4G Wild Weasel

The chief threat to US aircraft over Vietnam was not enemy aircraft but, rather, surface-to-air (SAM) missiles. During the 1960s, the USAF utilized the Wild Weasel III, built on the F-105F Thunderchief airframe, to combat this threat. As the decade ended, attrition had pointed to the need for a replacement built on a current-production airframe. Initially, thirty-six F-4Cs were converted to EF-4C Wild Weasel IV configuration, but that type was inadequate, the most notable deficiency being that it could not carry the necessary antiradiation missiles, which homed in on enemy radar.

The more capable F-4E aircraft would form the basis for the next attempt. To test the concept, a mock installation of the equipment needed to launch the AGM-78 Standard antiradiation missile was made on YF-4E 65-0713. The results were encouraging, and the decision was made to covert 116 low-time F-4E aircraft for use as anti-SAM aircraft. These would be code-named Wild Weasel V.

The aircraft, which were ultimately designated F-4G, were rebuilt from block 42 to block 45 F-4Es. The first of these, 69-7254, was modified by McDonnell Douglas and began test flights in December 1975. The remainder of the conversions were performed by the Air Force at Hill AFB, Utah, with the final conversion being completed in 1981.

The conversions involved removing the M61A1 cannon and ammunition drum and installing an under-nose fairing for forward and side-looking radar antennas. On the exterior of the aircraft, fifty-two receiving and emitting antennas were installed.

The aircraft were initially equipped to carry the AGM-45 Shrike and the AGM-78 Standard antiradiation missiles, both of which were later superseded by the Texas Instruments AGM-88 High-Speed Anti-Radiation Missile (HARM), and the F-4G was adapted accordingly.

In addition to the antiradiation missiles, the F-4G could be armed with the AGM-65 Maverick air-to-ground missile, the Mk. 84 electro-optical glide bomb, the homing-bomb system, and cluster weapons such as the Rockeye, CBU-52, and CBU-58.

For self-defense, the F-4G could carry up to four AIM-9 Sidewinder and four AIM-7 Sparrow air-to-air missiles. Typically, the Sparrow load was reduced by one to accommodate the installation of an ALQ-119 or ALQ-131 jammer pod.

Many of the above systems were controlled by the back-seat crew member, whose position had three primary displays: a plan-position indicator, a panoramic analysis display, and a homing indicator. With this gear, each threat—its range, bearing, and type—was shown on the display, and the threat deemed by the system to be the most dangerous is identified by having a bright triangle superimposed over it.

The F-4G became operational in April 1978. At the time of Desert Shield in 1991, two squadrons of the 35th TFW, the 561st TFS and the 562nd TFTS, were equipped with the F-4G. Twenty-four F-4Gs of the 561st TFS were deployed to the Middle East as part of Desert Shield. They played a key role in Desert Storm by suppressing Iraqi defenses during the initial attack on January 17.

The success of the aircraft during this action caused the previously planned transfer of all F-4G aircraft to Air National Guard units to be postponed, and a new active-duty USAF F-4G squadron, the 561st FS of the 57th FW, was activated at Nellis AFB. That unit would become the last active USAF Phantom squadron and was inactivated at Nellis AFB in March 1996, and its F-4Gs were placed in storage at Davis-Monthan AFB. The next month, the last F-4Gs were withdrawn from Air National Guard service, and they too dispatched to Davis-Monthan.

Thereafter, the only Phantoms flown on behalf of the US military were drones, most often used as targets.

To combat enemy surface-to-air (SAM) missile sites, the US Air Force developed the Wild Weasel concept: planes equipped to locate the radar emissions of SAM sites and destroy the sites with antiradiation missiles. To replace the dwindling numbers of F-105G Wild Weasels, in the 1970s the F-4G Wild Weasel was developed, of which 116 were converted from F4Es. Seen here is an F-4G armed with four AGM-45 Shrike antiradiation missiles on the wing pylons. *National Museum of the United States Air Force*

F-4E-43-MC 69-7254 was converted to a preproduction test aircraft designated the YF-4G. It was tested at Edwards AFB in 1976. The Vulcan gun was removed and replaced with a new fairing with forward and side-looking radar equipment. *National Museum of the United States Air Force*

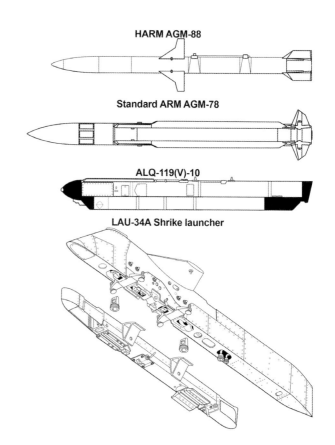

HARM AGM-88

Standard ARM AGM-78

ALQ-119(V)-10

LAU-34A Shrike launcher

The Wild Weasel Phantoms carried this array of ordnance.

F-4G 69-291, with the 81st Tactical Fighter Squadron, has twenty-six "spooks" on the splitter plate, representing twenty-six radar site kills in Desert Storm.

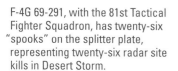

The only F-4G that was painted in the markings of the 192nd Fighter Squadron, Nevada Air National Guard "High Rollers." Reno, Nevada, 1991.

Col. Fryjack, commander of the 52nd Tactical Fighter Wing at Spangdahlem AB, Germany, flew this F-4G when the 81st Tactical Fighter Squadron redeployed back to Nellis AFB in 1996.

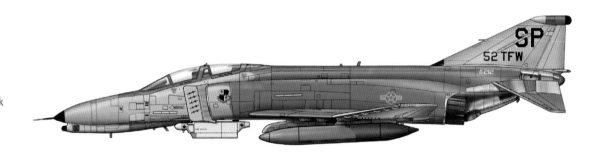

The F-4G was the final type to see use in a combat environment by the USAF, with the Wild Weasel Phantoms being retired in December 1995. During Desert Storm in 1991, forty-eight F-4Gs flew 3,942 combat sorties, firing 1,000 air-to-ground missiles and destroying 200 Iraqi missile sites.

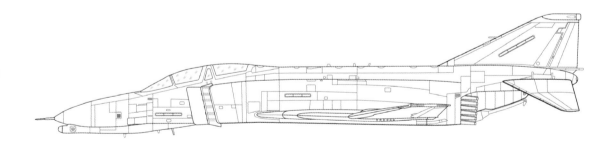

An F-4G is viewed head on, with a revetment to its rear. In the nose was an AN/APQ-120 radar. Below the nose is the chin radome of the AN/APR-38 radar-warning and attack system, which included a Texas Instruments reprogrammable computer. *National Museum of the United States Air Force*

Air Force personnel are prepping an F-4G for a flight. This plane carries a WW code on the vertical tail. Under the fuselage is an ALQ-119 electronic-countermeasures pod. At the top of the vertical tail is a streamlined fairing for the aft APR-38 high-band antenna. *National Museum of the United States Air Force*

F-4G 69-7584 is painted in a Southeast Asia camouflage scheme. The WW tail code was associated with F-4G Wild Weasels of several different squadrons. This plane was among the first of two lots of airframes converted to F-4Gs at the Ogden Air Logistics Center. *National Museum of the United States Air Force*

On the left inboard pylon is an AGM-65 Maverick air-to-surface missile, while the inboard right pylon carries an AGM-78 Standard ARM. On the left outboard pylon is an AGM-88 HARM antiradiation missile, with an AGM-45 Shrike antiradiation missile on the right outboard pylon. *National Museum of the United States Air Force*

The dark-colored object on the side of the chin fairing on an F-4G with USAF serial number 69-7301 is the left AN/APR-38 beam receiver. The black dome at the front of the fairing is for the forward receiver of the AN/APR-38 radar-warning and attack system. *National Museum of the United States Air Force*

An F-4G Wild Weasel coasts over mountainous desert terrain. A Maverick guided missile is visible on the inboard pylon. The F-4G was the final combat version of a Phantom II to see service with the US Air Force and Air Force Reserve. *National Museum of the United States Air Force*

The F-4G conversion involved removing the M61 cannon and replacing it with an AN/APR-47 electronic-warfare suite. The rear seat, rather than being occupied by a weapons system officer (WSO), was instead filled by an electronic-warfare officer (EWO). In addition to coordinating the firing of the of the AGM-88A/B/C High-Speed Anti-Radiation Missiles (HARM), the EWO also assisted with communications, as well as serving as navigator.

The last active-duty Air Force pilot to fly the McDonnell Douglas F-4 Phantom II, Lt. Col. Ron "Elvis" King, *right,* commander of the 82nd Aerial Target Squadron Detachment 1, talks with former QF-4 pilot Eric "Rock" Vold and a civilian QF-4E pilot/controller, Lt. Col. (Ret.) Jim "WAM" Harkins, after they piloted the final military flight of the storied aircraft at Holloman AFB, New Mexico, on December 21, 2016. *US Air Force photo by J. M. Eddins Jr.*

Pilots of 82nd Aerial Target Squadron Detachment 1 led the final military flight of the storied F-4 Phantom II at Holloman AFB, on December 21, 2016. The F-4 Phantom II entered the US Air Force inventory in 1963 and was the primary multirole aircraft in the USAF throughout the 1960s and 1970s. The F-4 flew bombing, combat air patrol, fighter escort, reconnaissance, and the famous Wild Weasel antiaircraft-missile-suppression missions. The final variant of the Phantom II was the QF-4 unmanned aerial target flown by the 82nd at Holloman AFB. *US Air Force photo by J. M. Eddins Jr.*

An iconic aircraft of the jet age, the F-4 Phantom II made a lasting impact from its first operational flights in 1960 until it was retired from US service in the mid-1990s, and it continues to serve in several foreign air forces. The Phantom proved to be a tough, durable, and highly versatile aircraft, able to more than hold its own in the aerial-combat, attack, reconnaissance, and SAM-suppression roles. From the Vietnam War to Operation Desert Storm, Phantoms left their mark. *National Museum of Naval Aviation*